AF593517

Unfamiliar Journeys
CONTINUED

Photographs by Alan McKernan

Text by Matthew Whitfield

First published 2008 by
Liverpool University Press
4 Cambridge Street
Liverpool
L69 7ZU

British Library Cataloguing-in-Publication data
A British Library CIP record is available

ISBN 978-1-84631-169-7

Designed by AW @ www.axisgraphicdesign.co.uk
Printed and bound by EBS, Verona

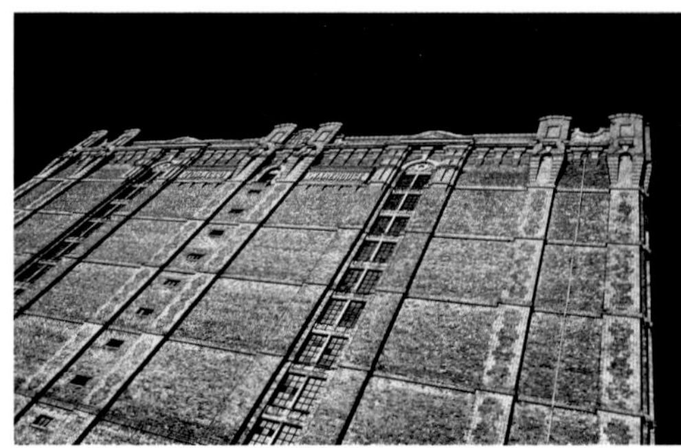

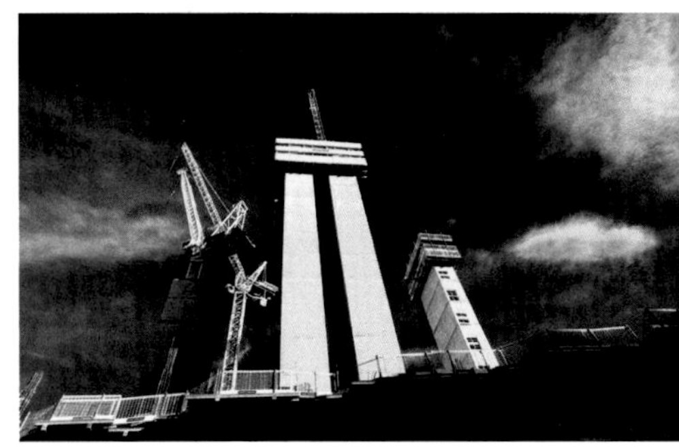

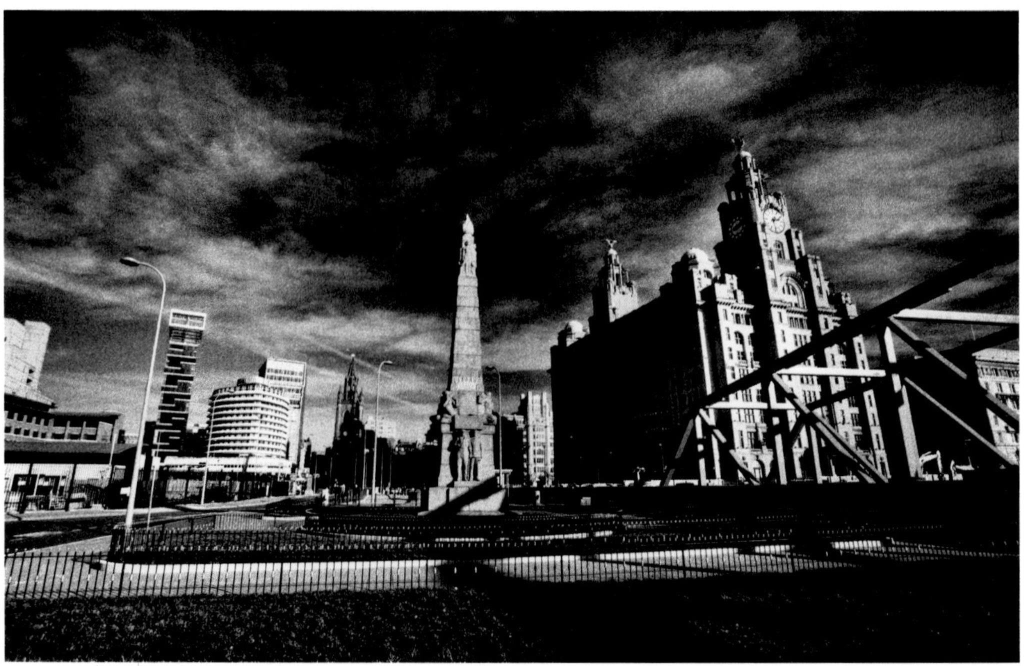

Contents

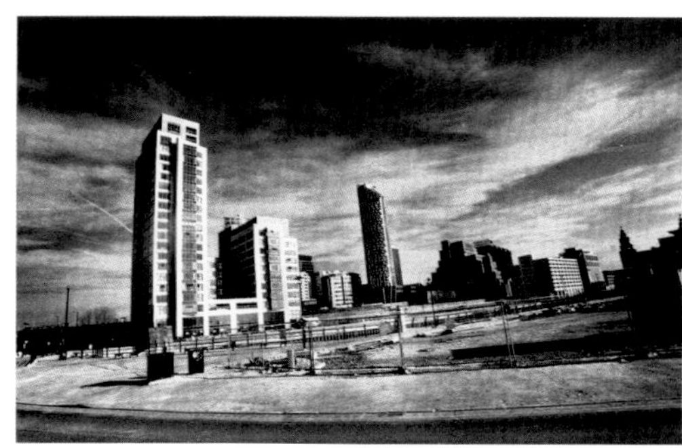

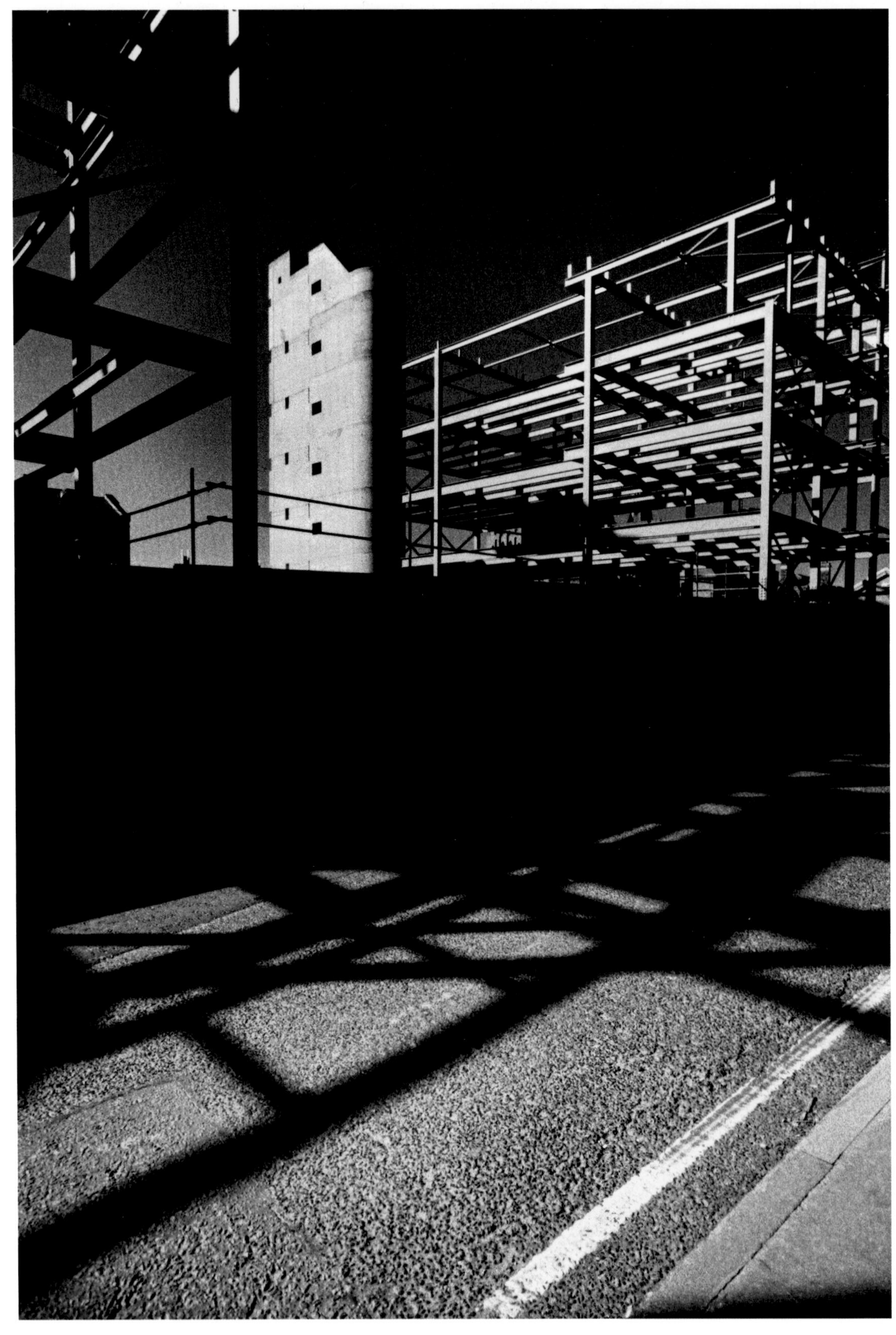

Preface

As a photographer, I've long been fascinated by, and experimented with, the ever-changing quality of light as it plays upon the cityscape of Liverpool, sculpting and re-defining it. I first explored the buildings of Liverpool in *Unfamiliar Journeys*; now, with this new selection of work, I have set my own interpretation of the interplay of architecture and light in the context of the broader currents of change within the city. Matthew Whitfield's text responds to my work and ties it to the processes of renewal and stasis that have defined Liverpool in this decade.

Since 2000, Liverpool's rising and developing skyline has come to symbolise a broader change in the buildings and streets of the city. A genuine economic revival underlies these shifts in Liverpool's architecture and streetscapes, but the images here look beyond the glib messages of regeneration to the actual process of change. The glittering skyscrapers are seen here in the full, glorious light of the Mersey shore, but so too is the turbulence of construction, the uneasy period of dug ground and clumsy hoardings that the city must endure through the course of its metamorphosis. Meanwhile, decaying architectural fragments stubbornly refuse to disappear, making their own claims for the city's past. In spite of the cranes and re-branding and the title of European Capital of Culture, Liverpool is not born again but stands instead among the triumphs and failures of its history. Some of this history feels distant and cannot be understood except through protection and interpretation. Some is fresh enough to be revived, or so vital that its essential spirit of modernity and usefulness never went away.

The light falls still on this metropolis perched on the Mersey somewhere between England and the world, but the shadows that are thrown alter all the time. These photographs mark a time of gathering strength, of mingled hope and anticipation. Liverpool will be rebuilt, but these images of change *are* the city, what it always was and what it might be.

Commercial

This is commercial Liverpool, a city reaching upwards in the early twenty-first century, attempting to find a future in the air just as the sea brought its fortunes to shore in the preceding three centuries. Where once this attempt took the form of the Royal Liver Building, stately granite rising up a reinforced concrete frame to reach domed towers and Byzantine flourishes that have symbolised an entire city ever since, now multi-tonal glass is the thing, and smooth, artful concrete when solidity is called for. Collectively, these towers of the old and towers for the new are citadels of hope, for they could never have been erected without the sense that the success they embody is real and that the further success they strive for would indeed come. Commercial imperatives dictate this logic, and so the progress that the city sees in the construction of the West Tower, St Paul's Square and all of the multifarious office developments of this decade is an indication, speculative but emphatic, that Liverpool's economy has a viable future.

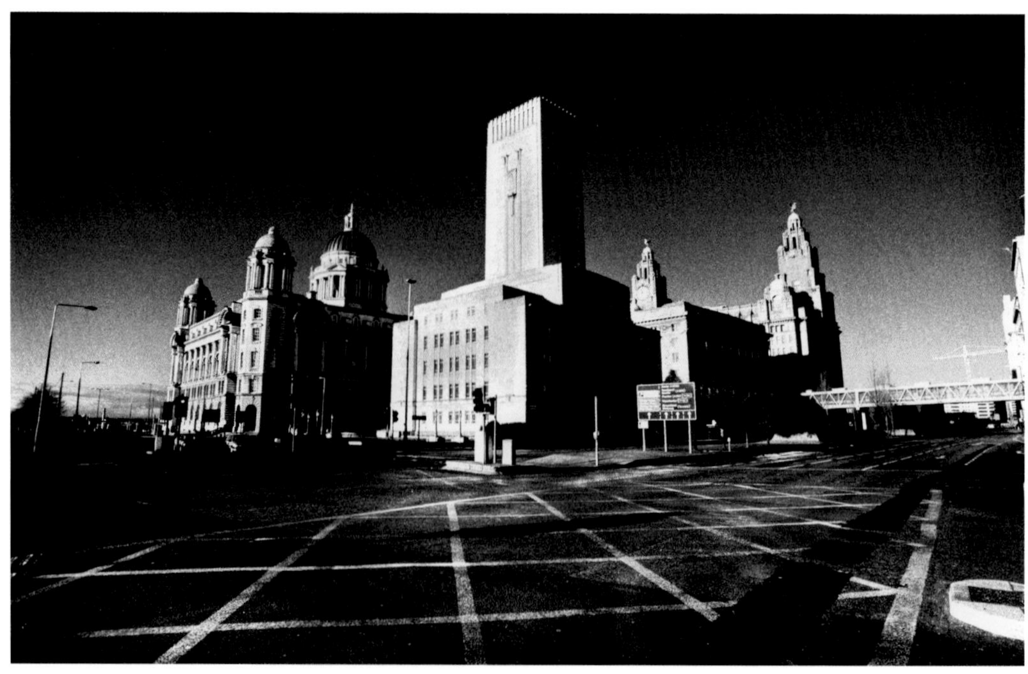

The thriving seaport of legend has long since slipped away, from a place where the produce, wealth, smells, culture and noise of the entire world was mingled into a cacophonous whole to a port whose annual tonnage passes through at a distance from the city's core and remains unnoticed. A switch in Britain's trading patterns towards the European Union and away from the Americas and Africa did not destroy Liverpool's trade with the world, but technological change radically altered the volume of the workforce required, while modern container ships required deep berths far downstream from the offices and shops of the central area. The ships and the dockers and the soot and the noise and the witnessed truth of Liverpool's existence – the things that could be seen – were moved, and for thirty or more years the city has evolved a new visual reality. Banking, insurance and legal services grew in importance alongside the swelling tide of goods spilling onto quaysides and into warehouses during the nineteenth century, but now it is these financial and professional industries that the everyday Liverpudlian and visitor to the city sees as one of the few visible forms of economic activity. The very fabric of the commercial buildings makes this possible; in their confidence and ambition a sense is affirmed that wealth was once created here and will be again.

Priorities change. History intercedes in the way of perfect progress. The Royal Liver Building, completed in 1911 during the lucrative salad days before the Great War, heralded an era of skyscrapers that never arrived. This most modern of office blocks represented the apogee of technical development which had progressed through the course of the nineteenth century, during which the possibilities of brick and stone were steadily stretched through the elasticity of cast iron, steel and glass. New technologies gave rise to larger windows, taller buildings and a gradual de-emphasis of decorative detail in favour of height, effective massing and, above all, function. Statements of style were made alongside this gradual revolution in structure, so that the voice of the classical world (or Renaissance Florence, Medieval England or any number of reflections of place and time) could be heard echoed in the modern metropolis of Liverpool. Not one of these styles gained exclusive ascendancy, as Liverpool was cast variously as the new Athens, Florence or Rome. Where once it was important to endow a commercial building with a solid stone portico using the language of Ancient Greece to speak with a certain gravitas, the more florid visions of the Italian Renaissance later took hold before the romantic nationalism of gothic gained approval, all during the course of one century. Relative economic decline from the mid-1930s onwards meant that the Royal Liver Building, instead of acting as a fulcrum between the technical innovation of the nineteenth century and the continuing process of modernist development in the twentieth century, instead stood as a monument to a certain moment of excited bombast.

New money, coupled with progress in engineering and computer-aided design, has set the scene for commercial buildings with an almost limitless capacity to fulfil the needs of owners and potential tenants. The material of the moment is glass, often used with an artistic flair that goes beyond the requirements of successful windows to produce a style all of its own. The tussle of stylistic imperatives that so defined the architectural landscape of the nineteenth century has today settled into a consensus that a commercial building will be welcomed so long as it subscribes to the essential modernist credo of well-serviced, functional space with no discernible applied style at all. Gloss – a certain shimmer – helps a good deal, too. If Renaissance Florence was the lodestar for Liverpool at a certain point in its self-confident past, it is now Shanghai, Sydney, Los Angeles (or any city that has played the game of hyper-capitalism and won) that offer the inspiration for the future.

This is commercial Liverpool now, in a moment. The towers of the old encourage the towers for the new, because office space wrapped crisply within glass in the sky represents a logical progression of everything that the innovators of the past stood for.

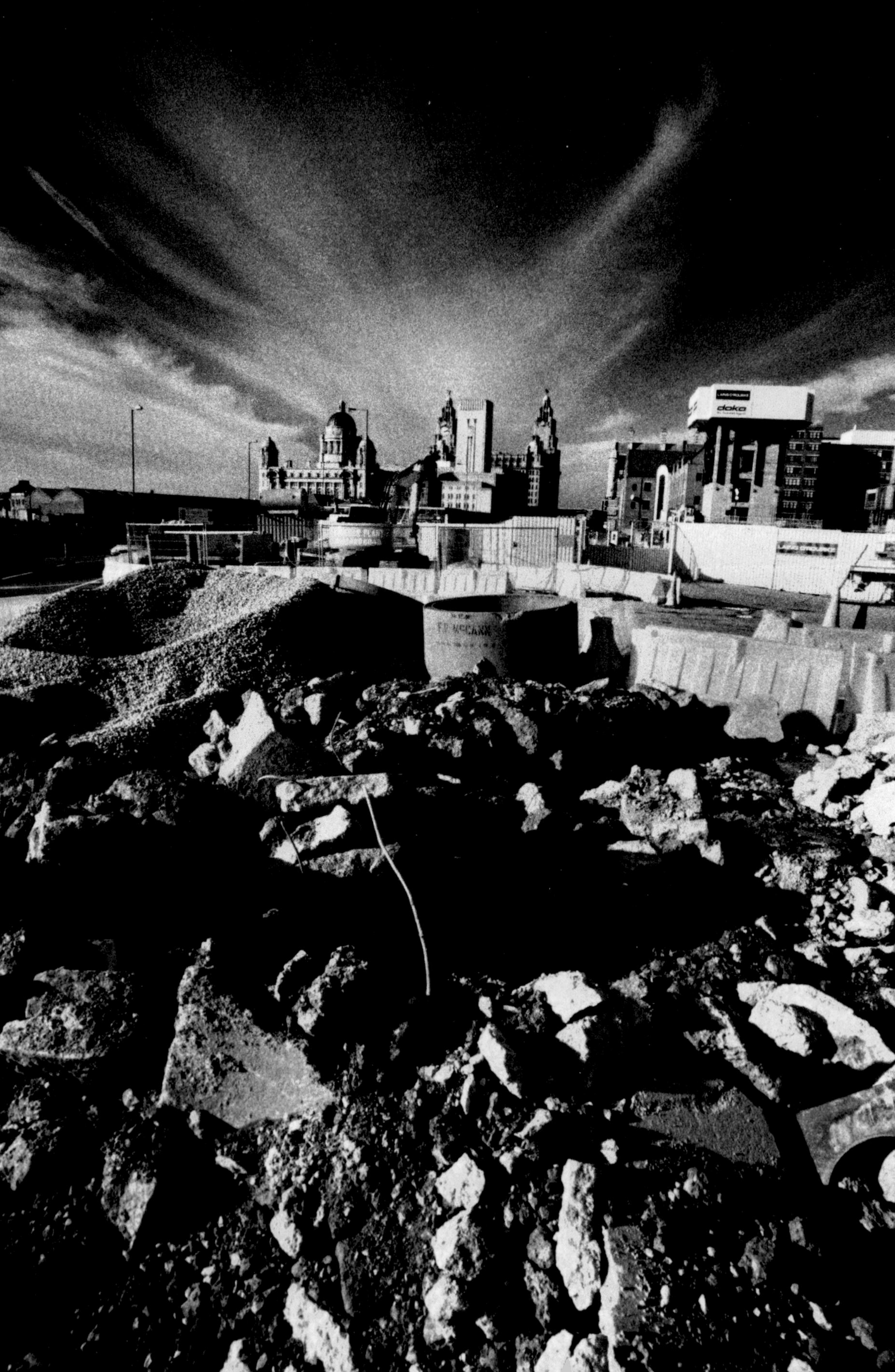

FEBRUARY 2007

Background from left to right: Port of Liverpool Building (formerly offices of the Mersey Docks and Harbour Board), Briggs and Wolstenhome/Hobbs and Thornley, 1903–07; Royal Liver Building, Walter Aubrey Thomas, 1908–11; George's Dock Ventilation Tower and Control Station, Herbert J. Rowse, 1932–34; One Park West under construction, César Pelli, 2006–08
Foreground: Roadwork excavations, Wapping

An aurora of cloud and vapour trails marks the site of the old city, up ahead across rocky ground. There is much to do to knit this metropolitan fabric back together. Roads, drains, pavements and car parks must be built, of course, for the city to move and function. One Park West will twist and glint over these new traffic flows, with apartments and offices overlooking a new park in one direction and the familiar forms of the Pier Head and Albert Dock in another. This is an alien landscape, the grit and rubble of the earth turned inside out, but it continues to move, it does not settle, and the man-made work will soon conquer the ground to make forms that announce their newness and utility.

FEBRUARY 2003

The Royal Liver Building is glimpsed from the centre of a vista filled with upward motion. Here, the city rises suddenly from the northern approach on Great Howard Street. The first Beetham Tower (under construction here on the right) began a twenty-first-century incarnation of the business quarter in which heights and ambitions were raised.

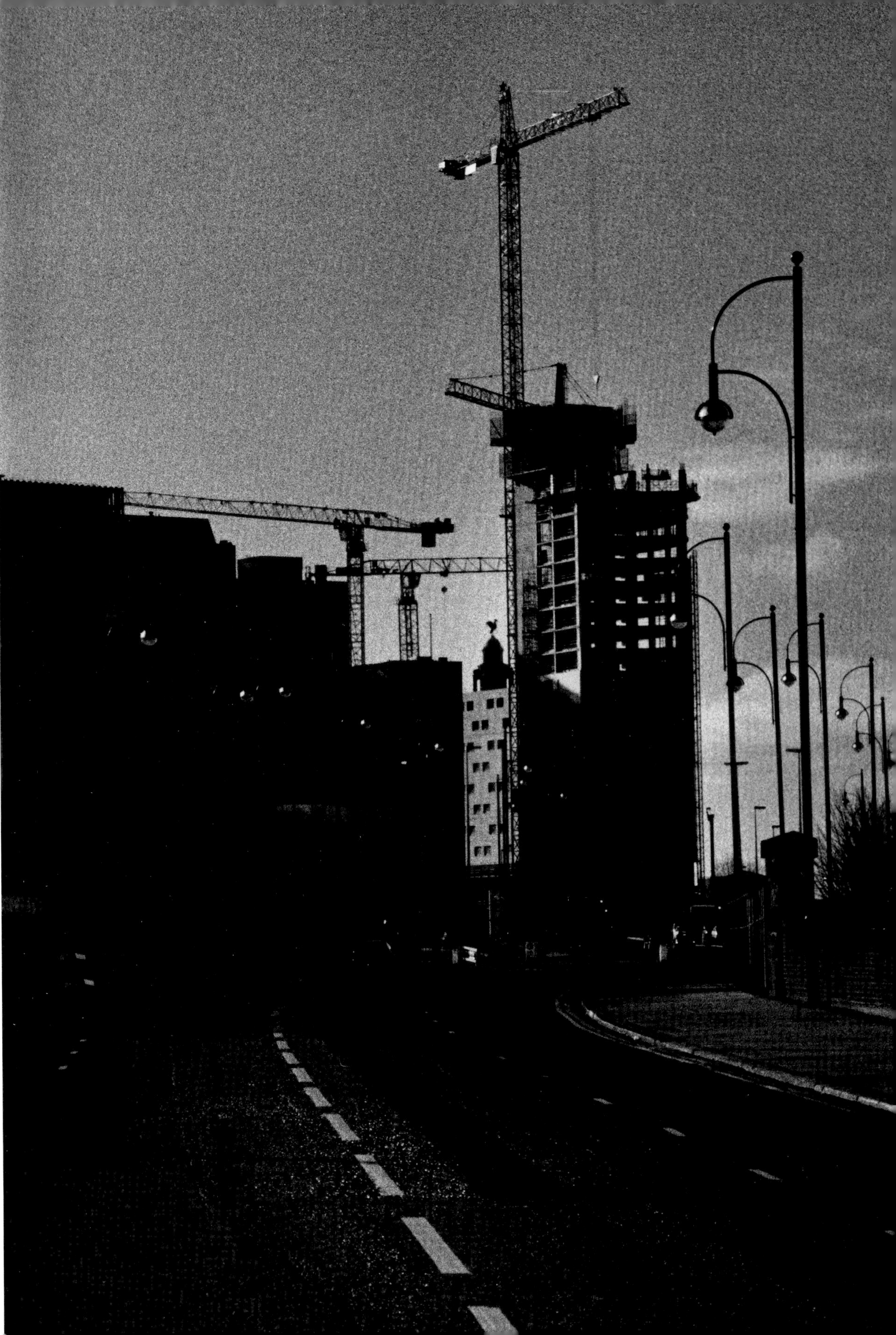

MARCH 2006

From left to right: Liverpool Daily Post and Echo building, Farmer and Dark, 1970–74; St Paul's Square under construction, RHWL Architects

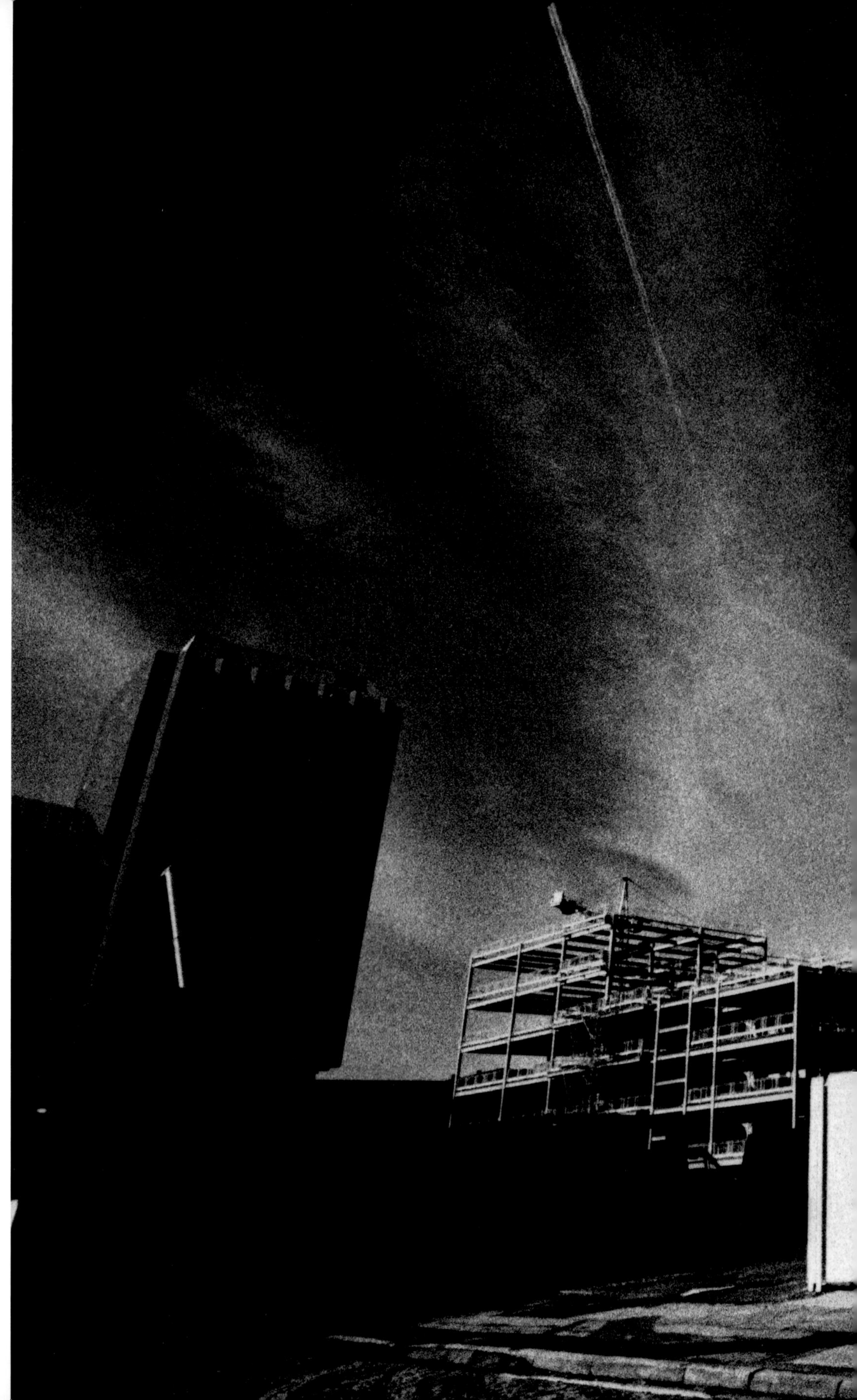

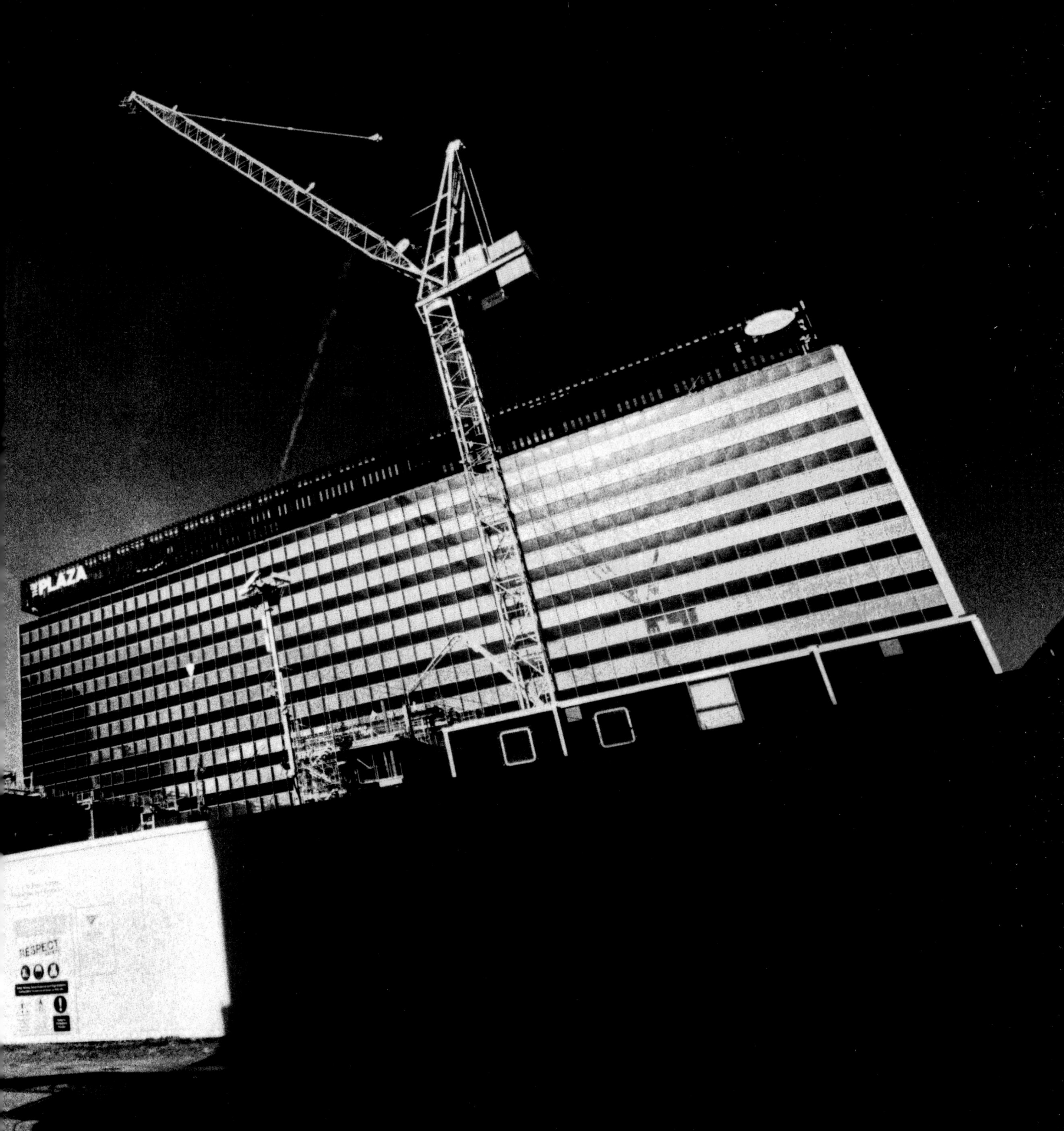
PLAZA
RESPECT

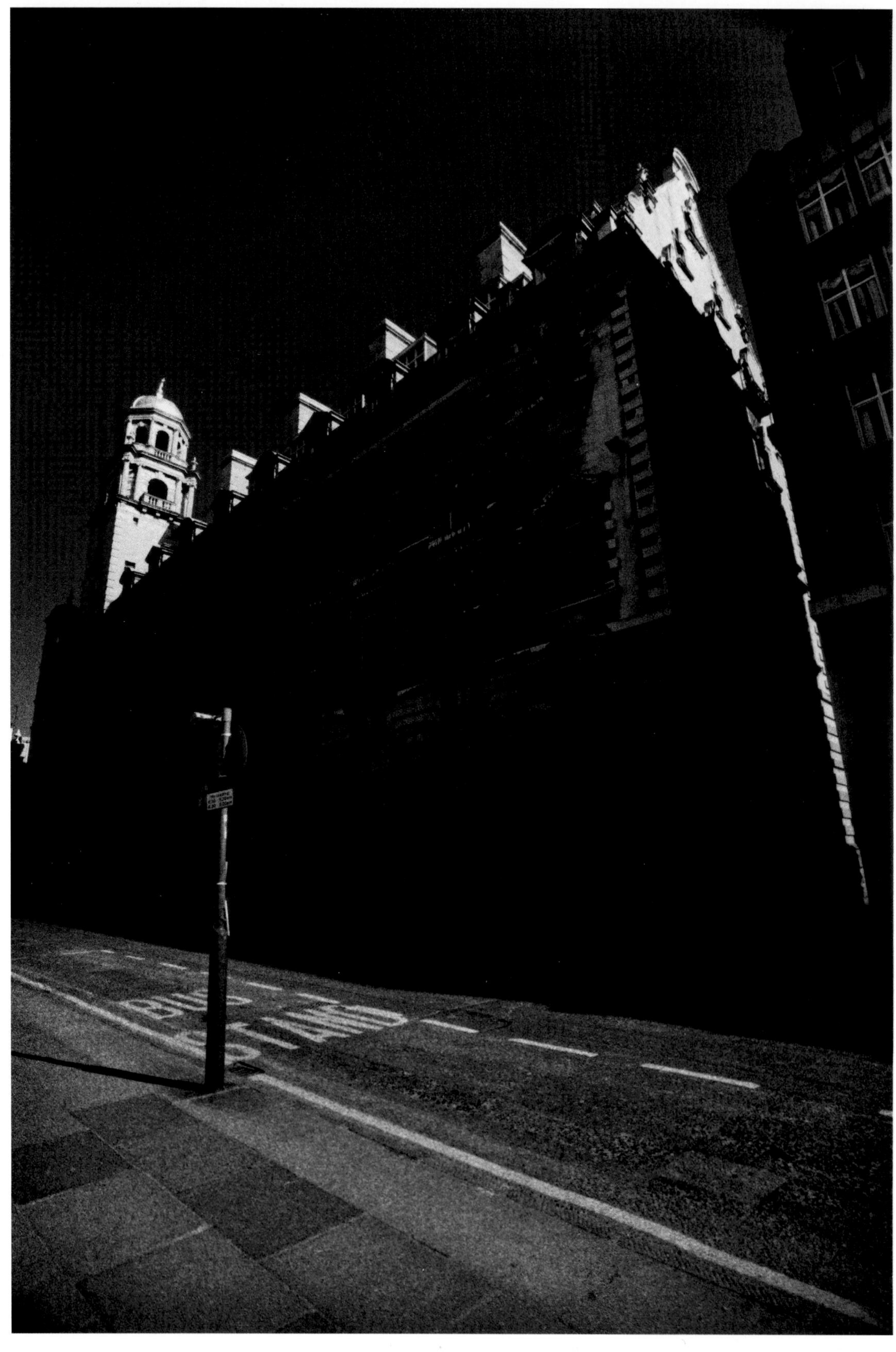

APRIL 2006

Former Royal Insurance head office, James F. Doyle, 1896–1903

APRIL 2007

From right to left: Cunard Building, Willink and Thicknesse, 1914–16; Royal Liver Building, Walter Aubrey Thomas, 1908–11; West Tower under construction, Aedas Architects, 2005–07

A deep line is scraped into the Pier Head, as though a deity from above has searched clumsily for traces of the eighteenth-century George's Dock that existed on this site. The preliminary excavation is part of the work on the Leeds and Liverpool Canal extension which, when completed, will partly resurrect that memory by bringing water back to this part of the dock system. The steel barrier, so definite in its task, separates the buildings of the Pier Head and their self-confident flourishes from the exercise in tourism and nostalgia on the other side. In the distance the real city grows again in the slight, translucent form of the West Tower, without the need for a new old canal.

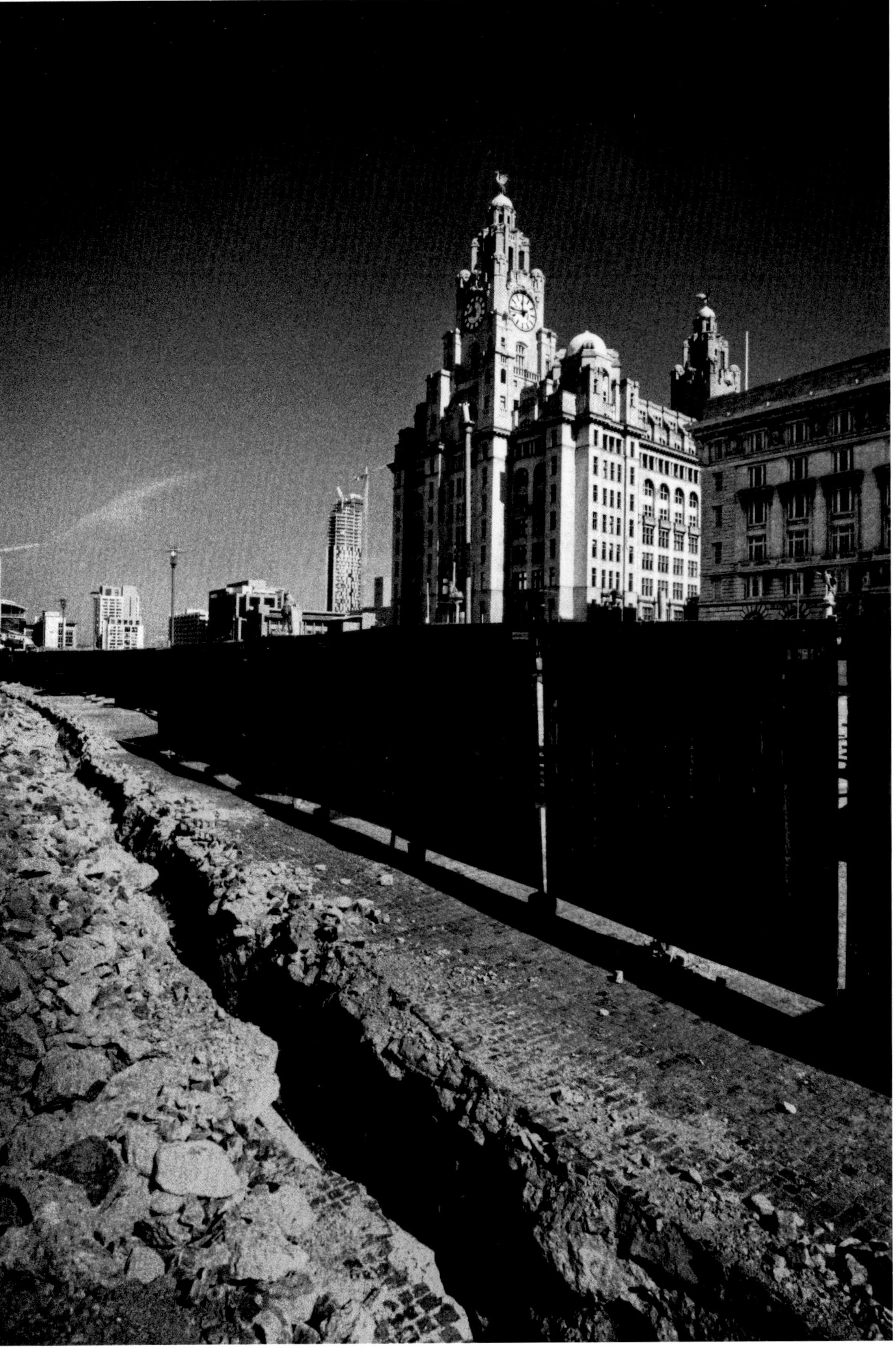

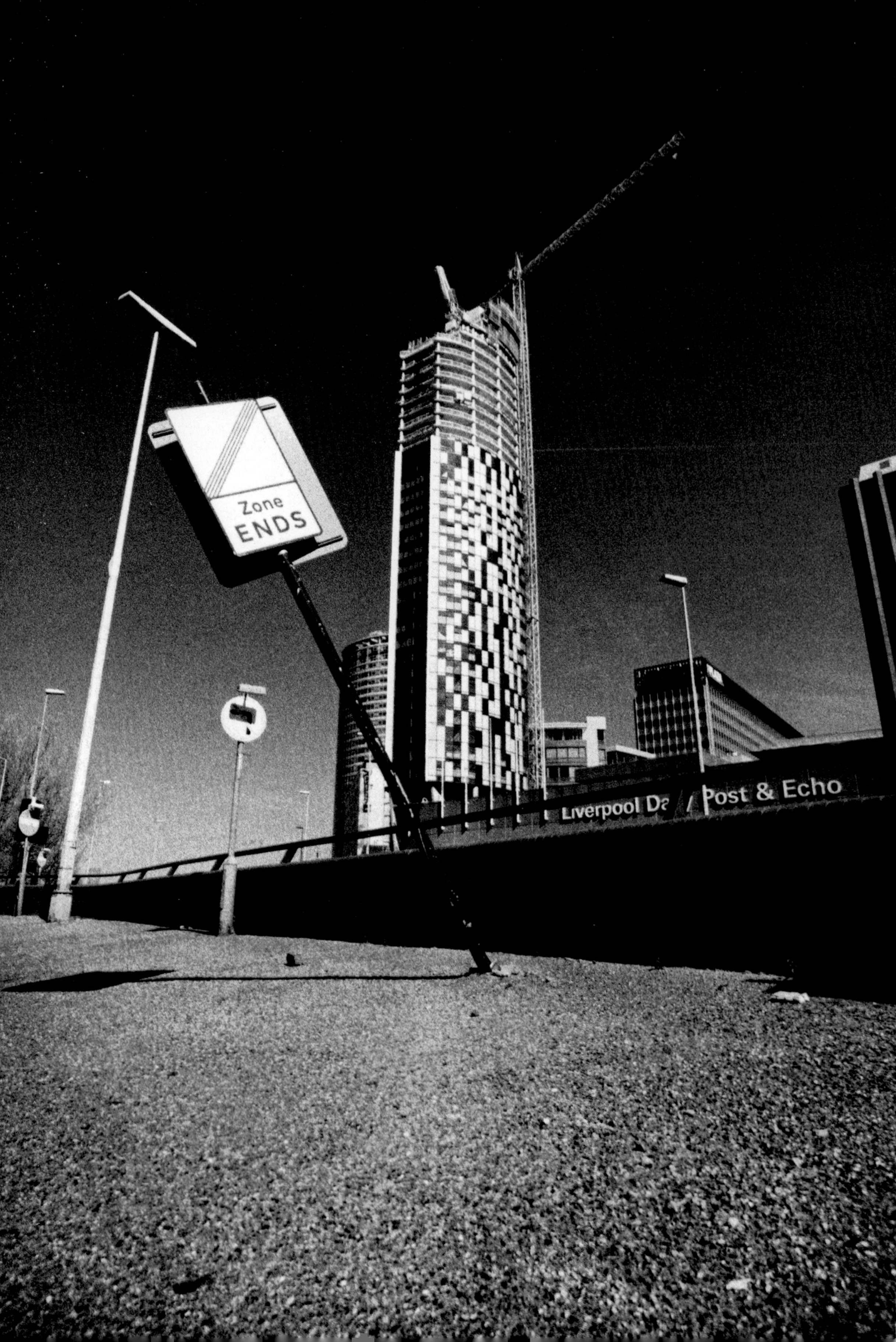

APRIL 2007

From left to right: Beetham Tower, Abbey Holford Rowe, 2004; West Tower under construction, Aedas Architects, 2005–07; The Plaza, formerly headquarters of Littlewoods plc, W.L. Stevenson for Littlewoods Department of Architecture & Planning, 1962–65; Liverpool Daily Post and Echo building, Farmer and Dark, 1970–74

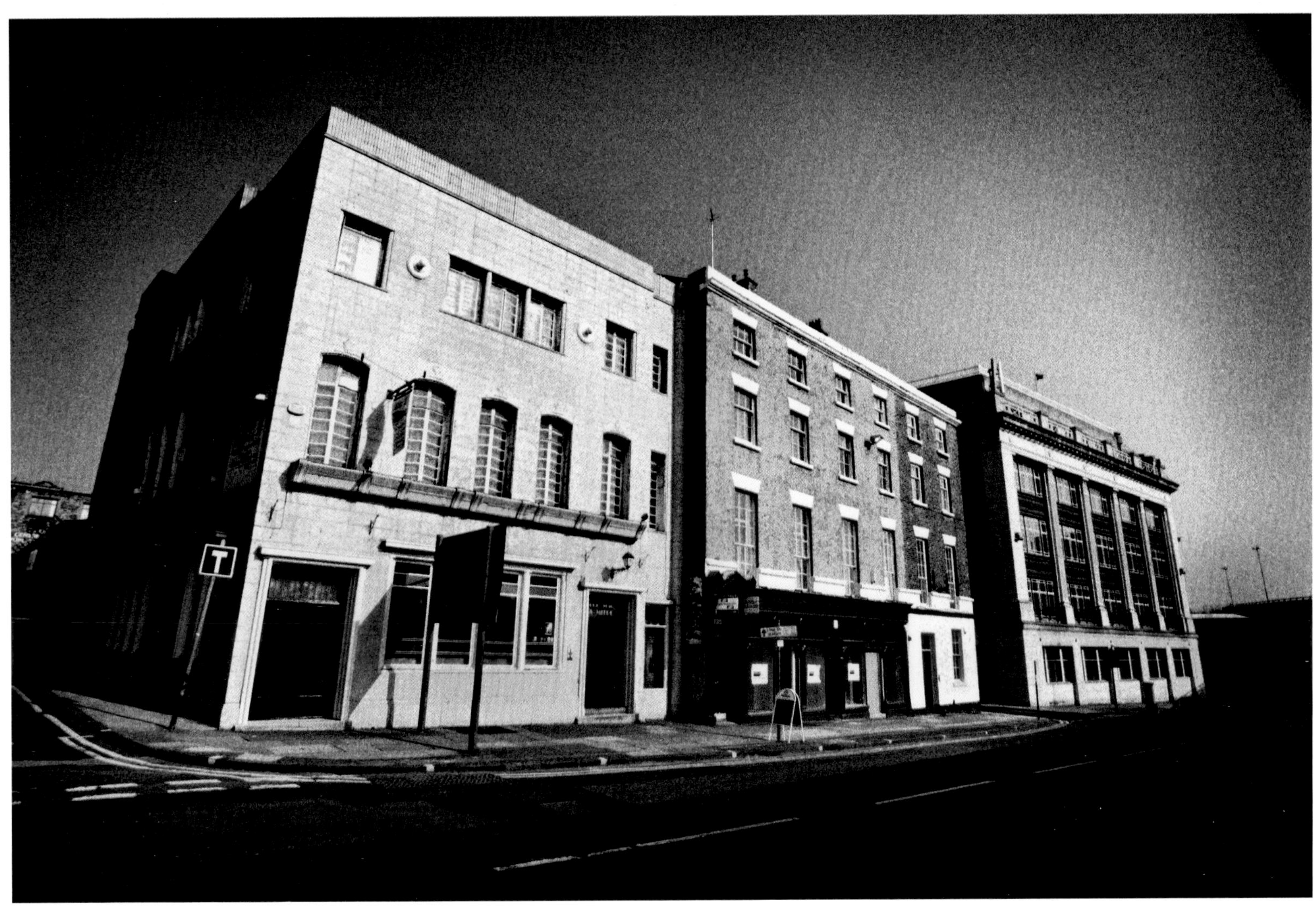

APRIL 2007

From left to right: Ship and Mitre public house; numbers 135–139 Dale Street, the only surviving eighteenth-century houses in the commercial quarter; former Blackburne Assurance Company, William P. Horsburgh, c.1932

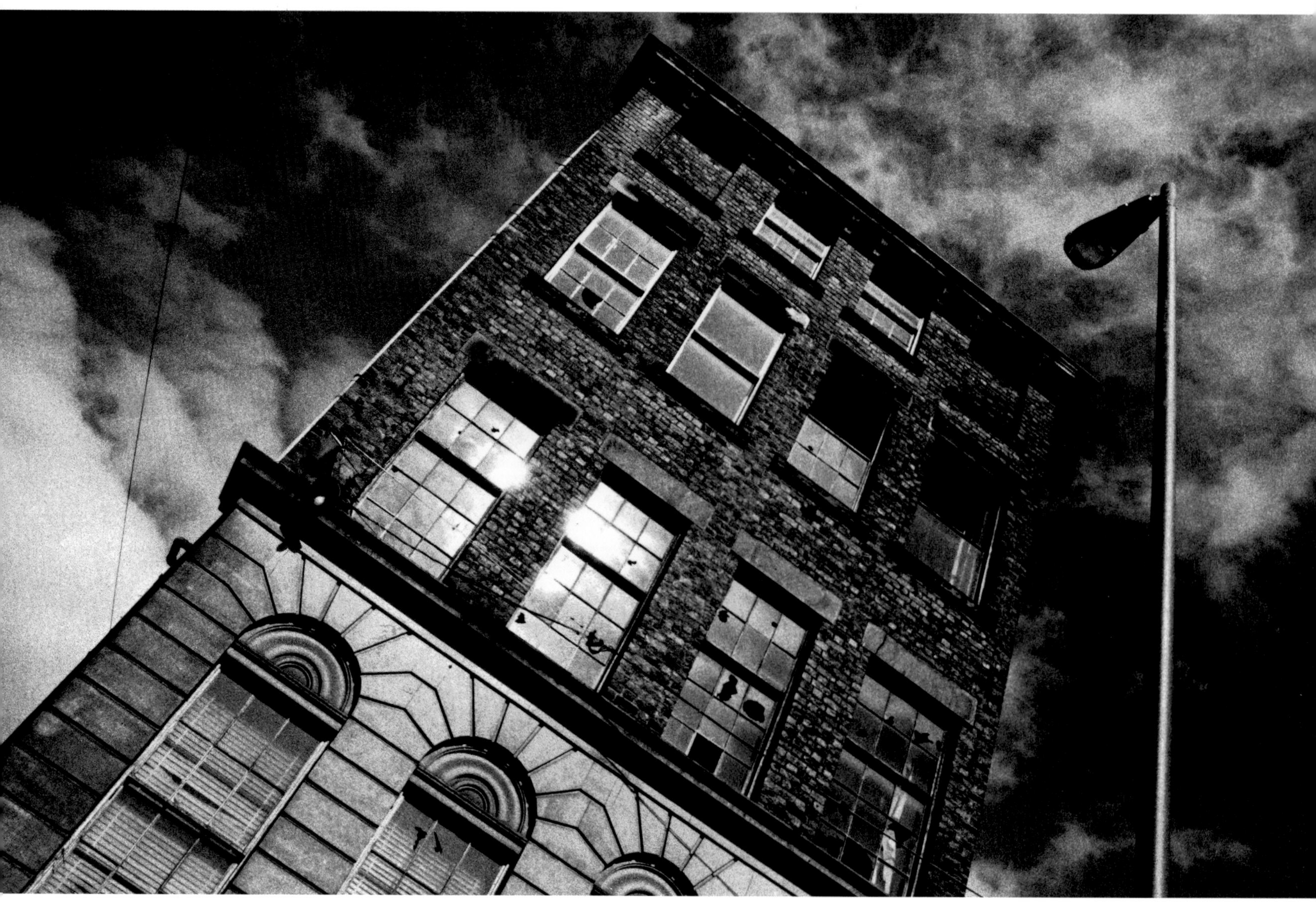

APRIL 2001

Office building for Rowlinson Brokers, Tempest Hey, William Culshaw, 1849

A proud survival, and surreally so in a street with no other remaining buildings, just rubble-strewn car parks. This handsome slice of Victorian streetscape survives the loss of its street with sheer grace under pressure. Future economic buoyancy may bring neighbours once more, but however welcome this would be, the end of this stage in the life of the building would be something of a loss.

MAY 2001

Clockwise, from bottom left: Buildings built c.1800 as part of Mr Clark's coal yard, alongside a former basin of the Leeds and Liverpool Canal; Lancaster House Telephone Exchange, 1936; The Plaza, formerly headquarters of Littlewoods plc, W.L. Stevenson for Littlewoods Department of Architecture & Planning, 1962–65

Three commercial eras come together for an eerie meeting. What they have to say to each other is difficult to determine, speaking as they do their separate languages. The muscular, stripped, corporate height of the Littlewoods building has little enough in common with the art deco organics of the telephone exchange of thirty years earlier, let alone the canalside cottages of the early nineteenth century. It is these earliest buildings that cause the most disquiet. They survived into the twenty-first century on a commercially viable site that would have seen them swept away in an economy more stable than Liverpool's. Now standing on the site of Beetham Tower and 101 Old Hall Street, restored fragments of the buildings survive, integrated into a hotel bar. This is less about conservation than the creation of a monument. Now the oddity of their existence is preserved, incongruously and unconvincingly, at the very centre of what should be Liverpool's vital economic heart.

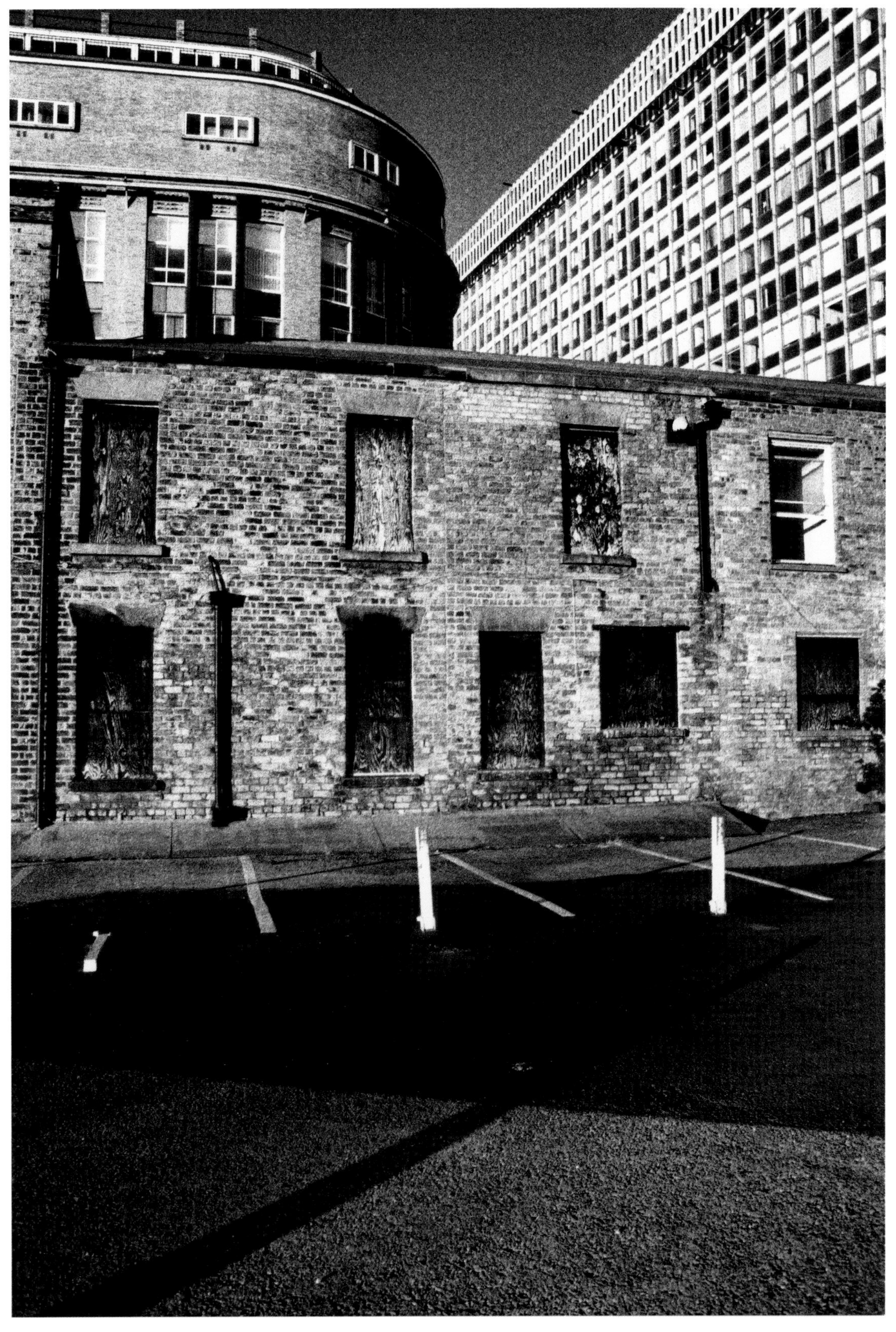

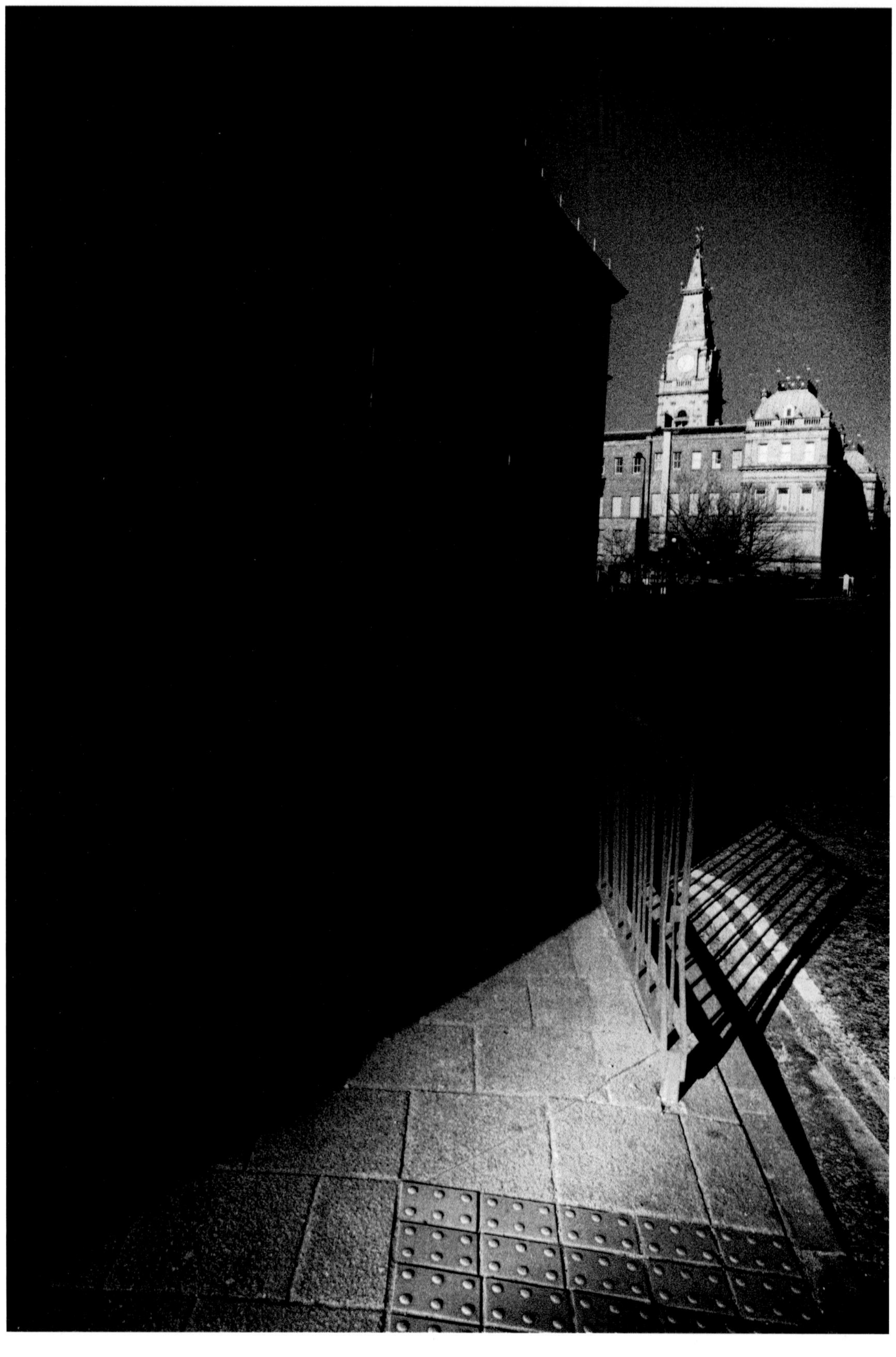

FEBRUARY 2005

Left to right: (silhouetted) National Conservation Centre, formerly Midland Railways goods warehouse, Culshaw and Sumners, 1872–74; Municipal Buildings, John Weightman & E.R. Robson, 1862–68

JUNE 2005

Water Street, as seen from the steps of India Buildings, Arnold Thornley and Herbert J. Rowse, 1924–30

Background, from left to right: Norwich House, Edmund Kirby and Sons, 1973; former Martin's Bank building, Herbert J. Rowse, 1927–32; dome of Liverpool Town Hall, James Wyatt, 1802

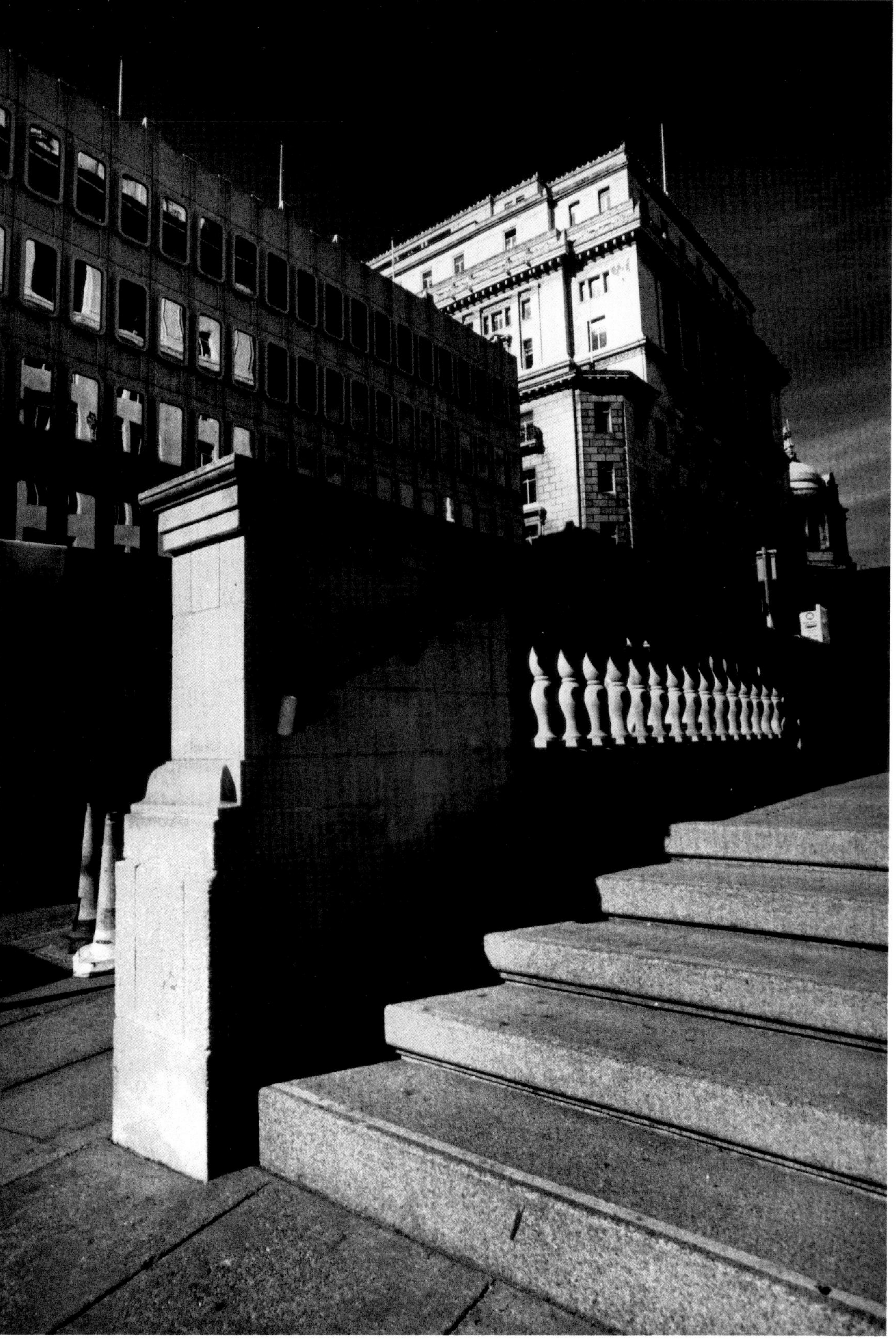

APRIL 2003

Across the dense cityscape of largely Victorian buildings rises the skyline of the post-war period.

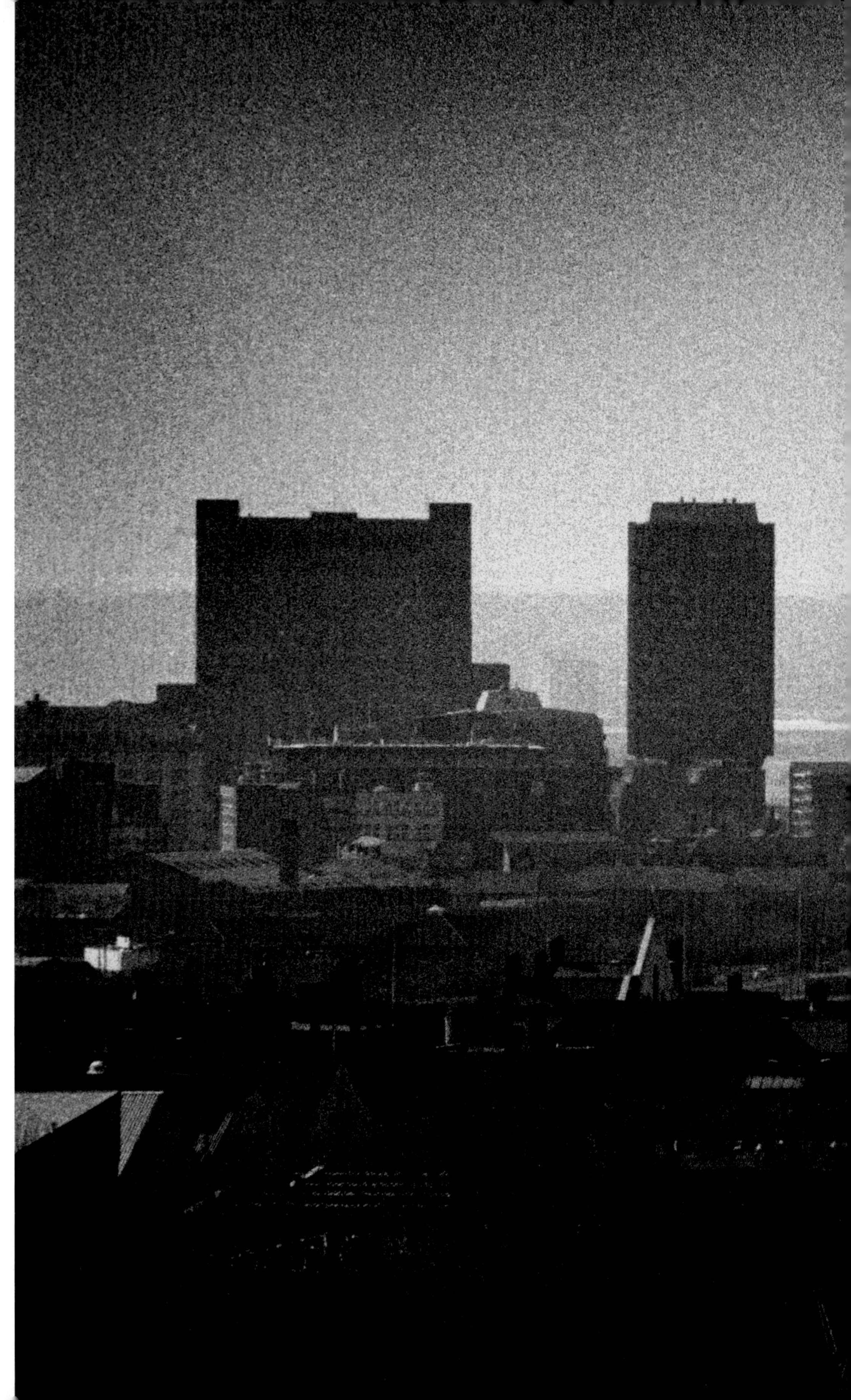

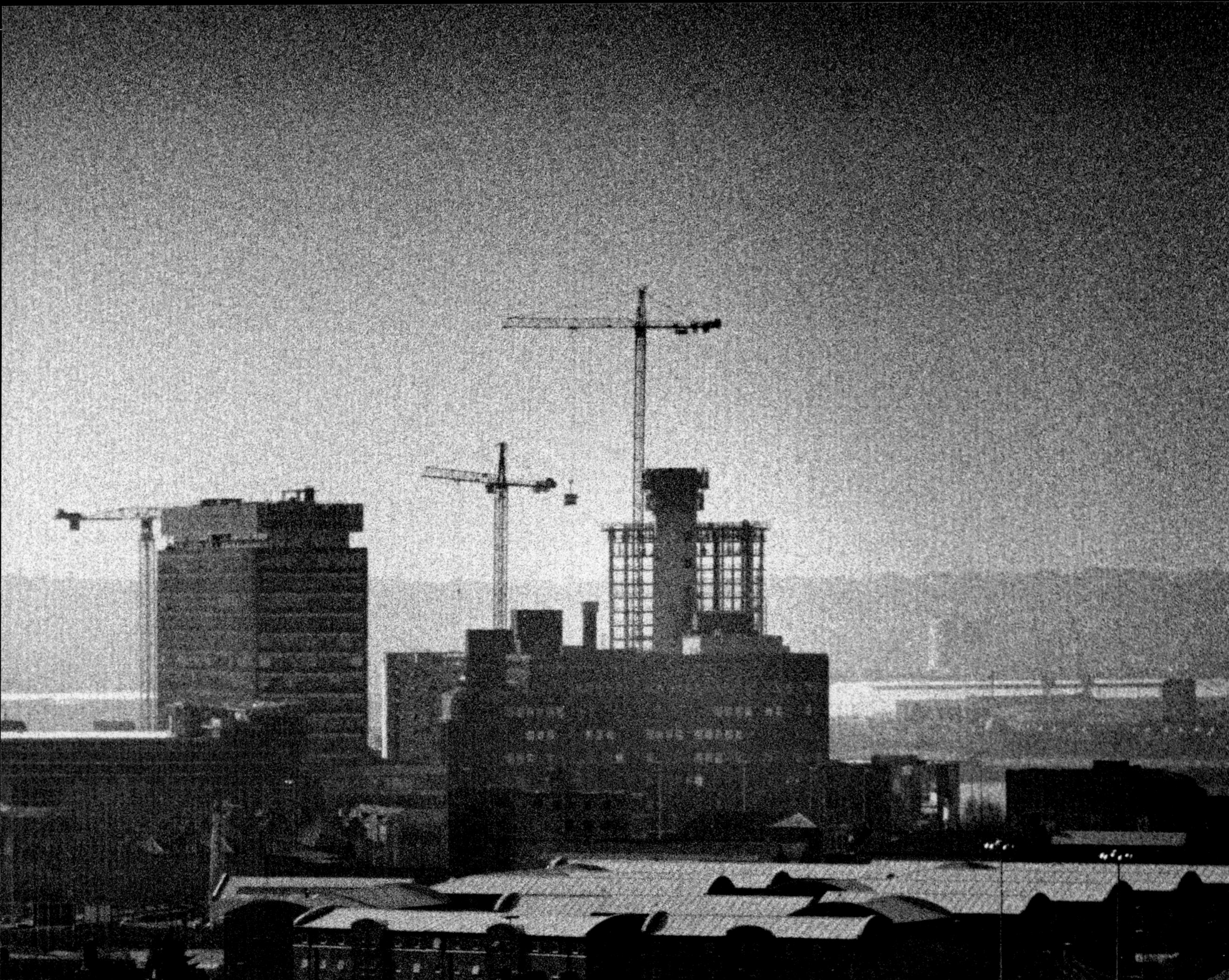

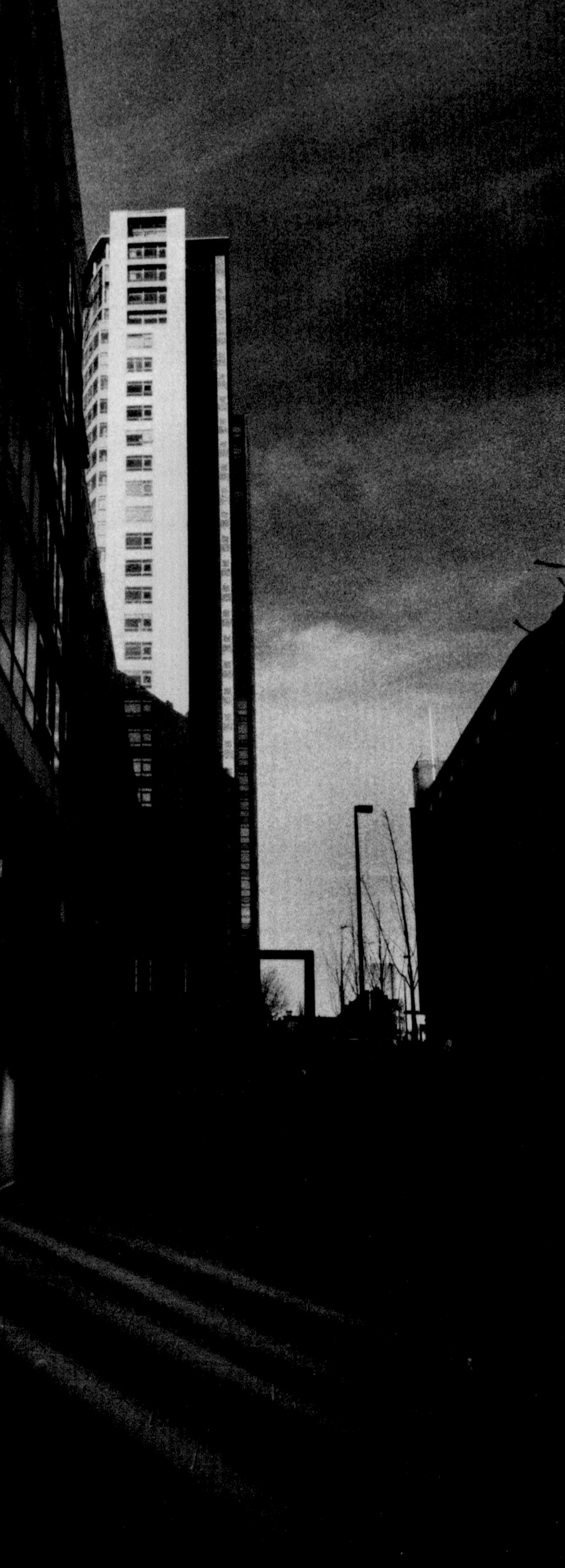

JANUARY 2007

101 Old Hall Street and Beetham Tower, Abbey Holford Rowe, 2004

APRIL 2004

Beetham Tower, Abbey Holford Rowe, 2004

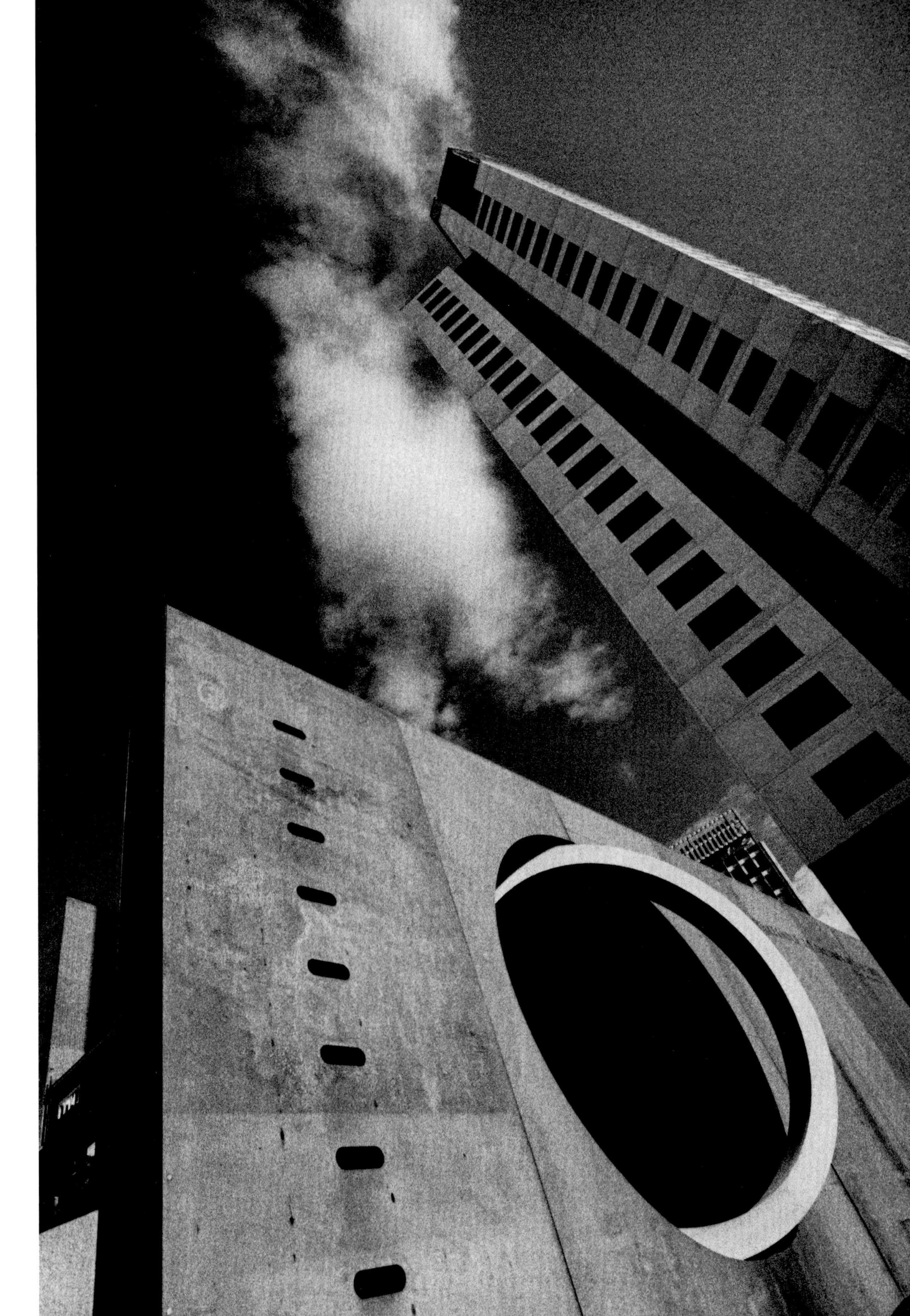

Home

Architecturally, Liverpool has a richness and depth that compares favourably to many of the great cities of Europe, perhaps even the world. Facing out towards the River Mersey and beyond to the trading routes of the Irish Sea, the Atlantic Ocean and, ultimately, the entire globe, the city has layered commercial function and noble ornament in its buildings to present a proud, heady image to the world. As much as this is a city of extraordinary endeavour, with a range of extraordinary public and commercial buildings that memorialise past achievements and say so much about the essential spirit of the place, it is also a place where innumerable people of the British Isles and other parts of Europe have made their home. This might be considered the most basic function that a city should fulfil, to provide somewhere for people to live, but without it every piece of civic grandeur would be for nothing.

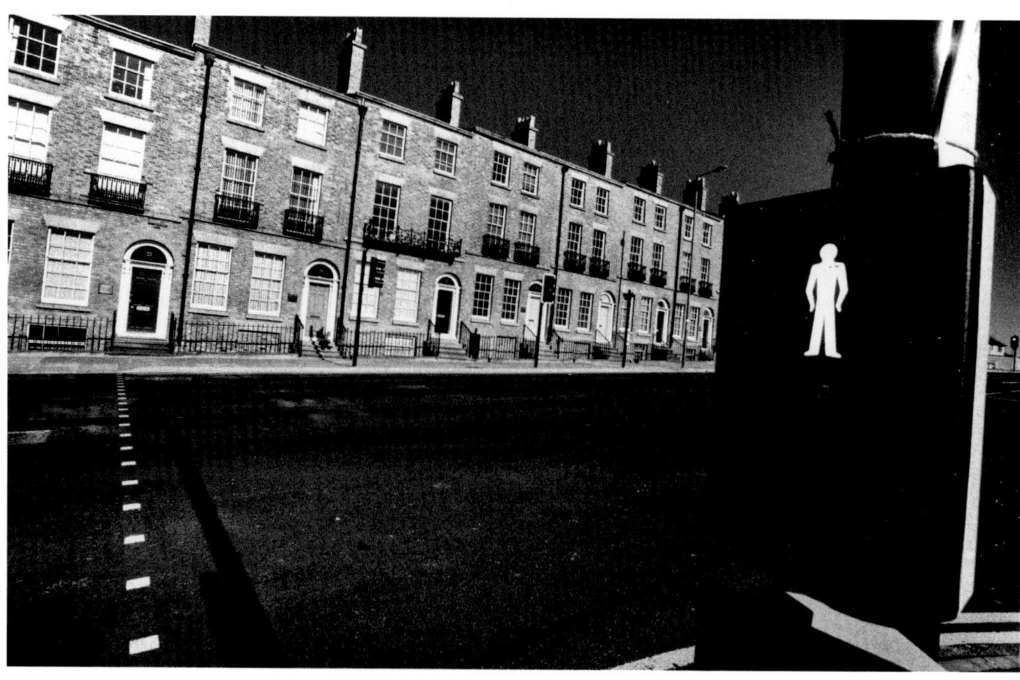

Through all of the romance of the city's setting on the Mersey, through the theatre of the Pier Head buildings and the cathedrals, the miles of docks and the superb gravitas of public buildings such as St George's Hall and the Town Hall, it is perhaps easy to lose sight of the fact that Liverpool is also a place of hearth and home. It is a place where meals are put on the table and laundry is done, where family units are formed and move through the generations, a place where rich and poor have gathered together and created a society, a mixture of class and ethnicity, that is all Liverpool's own. The city has gained a significant place in the national (and, indeed, international) consciousness as a place of cultural wealth and past glories, of strife and intransigence, of distinctiveness and difference. This is a part of England that feels far from English, and so in thinking about the everyday life of the city it is possible to imagine that it differs considerably from whatever constitutes normal everyday life elsewhere in the country. In a city built on movement and the looking outwards towards different lands, the idea of settlement or home can appear something of a paradox.

Nevertheless, this is a city as filled with houses, flats and other dwellings as any other. There is indeed a normality to Liverpool that belies its status as 'extraordinary'. There is a common misconception that the city has lost half of its population since the 1930s, when the first of many economic shocks hit and Liverpudlians began to move anywhere there was work, generally in a southwards direction. Though this trend was indeed real enough, the extent of outward migration can be misunderstood if one looks only at the housing patterns of the city of Liverpool and ignores the greater metropolitan area of Merseyside. Whereas cities such as Manchester and London are often thought of as constituting the sum total of their 'greater' metropolitan areas, and a city like Birmingham has an expansive city boundary that incorporates many outlying suburbs, Liverpool has been viewed as shrinking fast when in fact the greater Merseyside area has seen much less dramatic decline.

It is also a city with similar patterns of housing development as elsewhere in England, with one or two distinctive exceptions. There are many more Georgian terraces here than you would find in other large cities such as Leeds, Manchester or Birmingham, and perhaps an unusually high concentration of late nineteenth-century two-bedroomed terraces. Liverpool led the way in clearing its central slums in earnest from the inter-war period onwards and innovated in its extensive re-housing schemes. From the brick-built five-storey tenement flats of the 1920s and 30s to the concrete system-built point blocks of the 1960s, there has been a multiplicity of public schemes to upgrade living conditions, shift populations around the city and change the architectural form of the place in the process. Such trends are of course not unique to Liverpool but it was Liverpool that executed them in perhaps a more spirited and extensive manner than any other equivalent city.

These photographs explore a selection of the diversity in the city's housing stock and offer a glimpse of the many sites that Liverpool's citizens have at at one time or another called home. There is both the the restored and the ignored here, and new ideas jostling alongside the established, characteristic ways of living. Layers of regeneration are visible in the images, from the unreconstructed dwellings awaiting money or oblivion to replacement housing itself now restored, and everything in between.

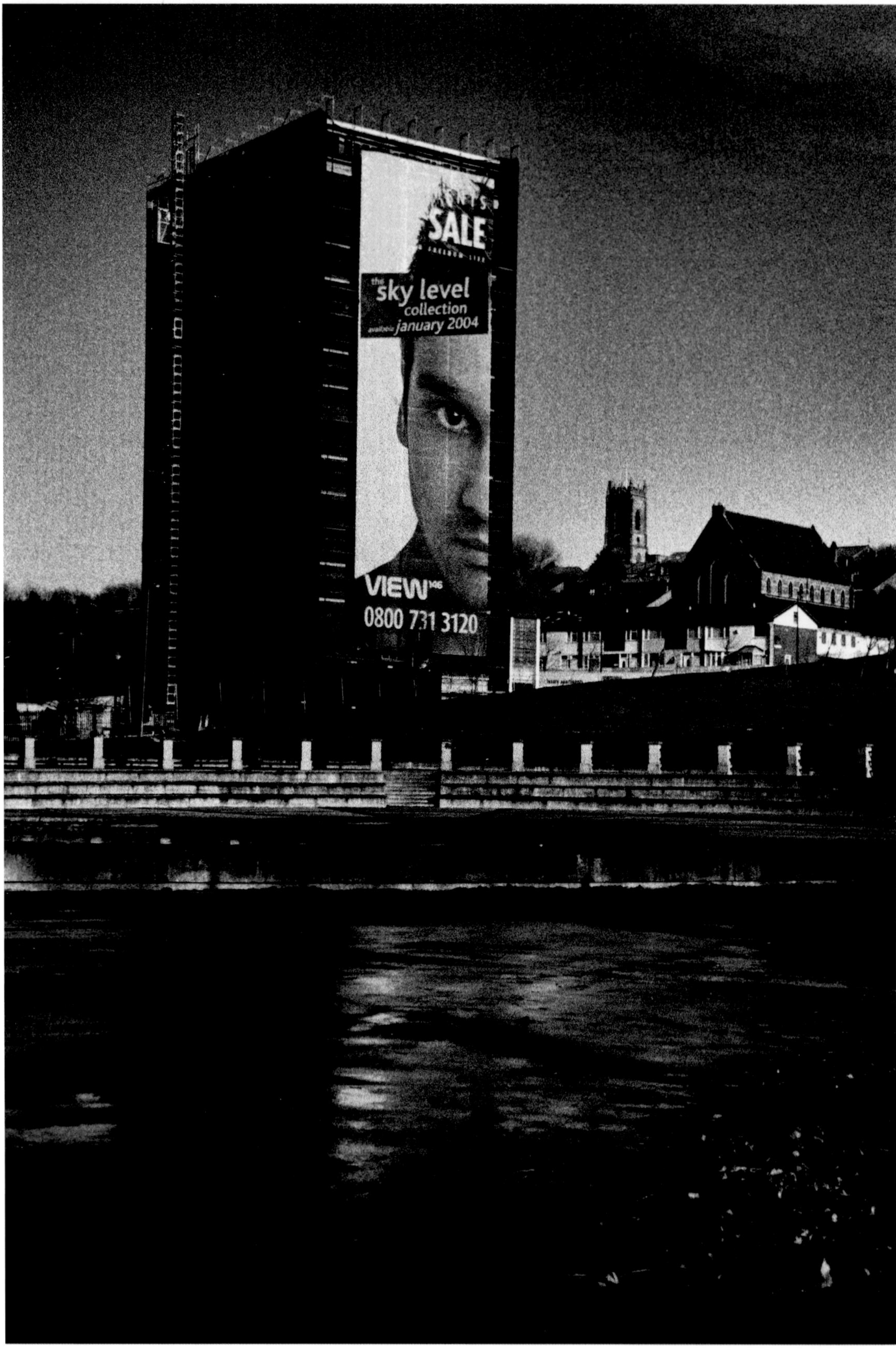

DECEMBER 2003

From left to right: 'View 146', redevelopment of former Millburn Heights (Liverpool City Council Architects Department, 1965) by LPC Living, 2003; St George's Church, Heyworth Street, John Cragg with Thomas Rickman and J.M. Gandy, 1813–14; St Polycarp, Netherfield Road North, George Bradbury, 1886

Prefabrication has a long pedigree in Liverpool. John Cragg erected St George's Church, its tower visible towards the centre of this image, largely using cast-iron components from his Mersey Iron Foundry during the early nineteenth century. The technological and artistic ambition that drove such a laudable project may be considered less obvious in the programme which brought forth Millburn Heights and the rest of the system-built tower blocks constructed by the city council during the 1960s and the years either side of that decade. Here, prefabrication was used to cut costs and to provide as many new homes as possible in the shortest period of time. Fundamentally, there was nothing wrong with these new homes as architecture, but a series of complex social and economic factors at large in the Everton district by the 2000s saw the tenure of this block pass first to a private company running the flats as accommodation for asylum seekers and, by 2003, to a property development firm which converted Millburn Heights into a luxury apartment scheme.

DECEMBER 2005

Olive Mount Heights (now demolished) and neighbouring housing, Wavertree

Liverpool has experimented with a variety of social housing solutions in the post-war period. Here, where point blocks meet terraces from the 1950s, the striking difference of scale is indicative of the breadth of the re-housing programme. This site in Wavertree has since 2005 been redeveloped again into a completely low-rise streetscape of two-storey houses.

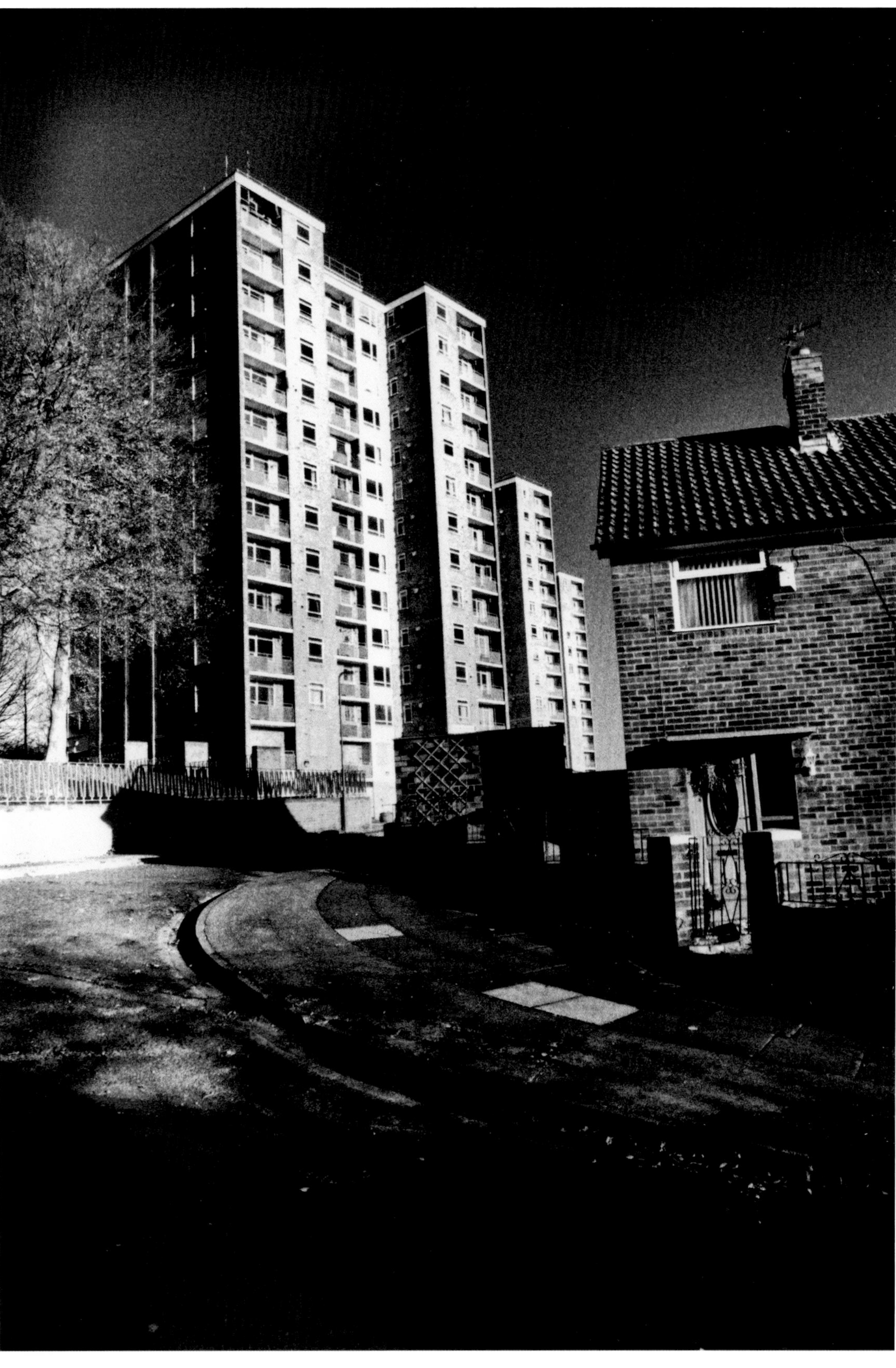

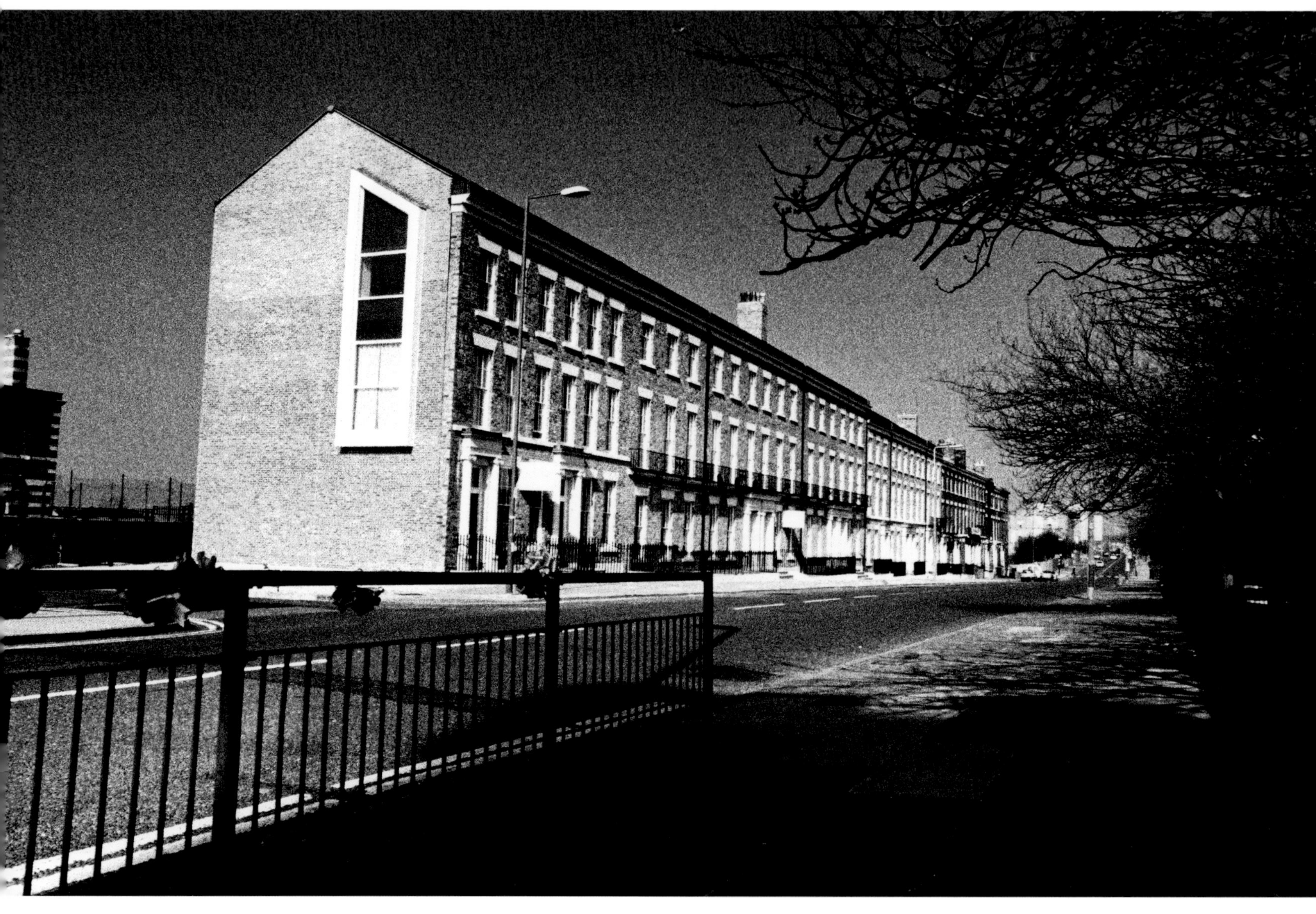

MARCH 2003

Terraced housing on Shaw Street, Everton, c.1830s

Restored during the early part of this decade, Shaw Street begins once again to resemble its past status as a street in a suburb of some repute. There has been much work along these lines in the Liverpool of the twenty-first century, taking the discarded remnants of the past, their survival scarcely believable, and giving them a fresh chance as though total dereliction had not happened. The insertion of a tall window in the end elevation is the clue offered by this building that, behind the façade, almost complete reconstruction has replaced the original accommodation. A version of the old Everton is living again.

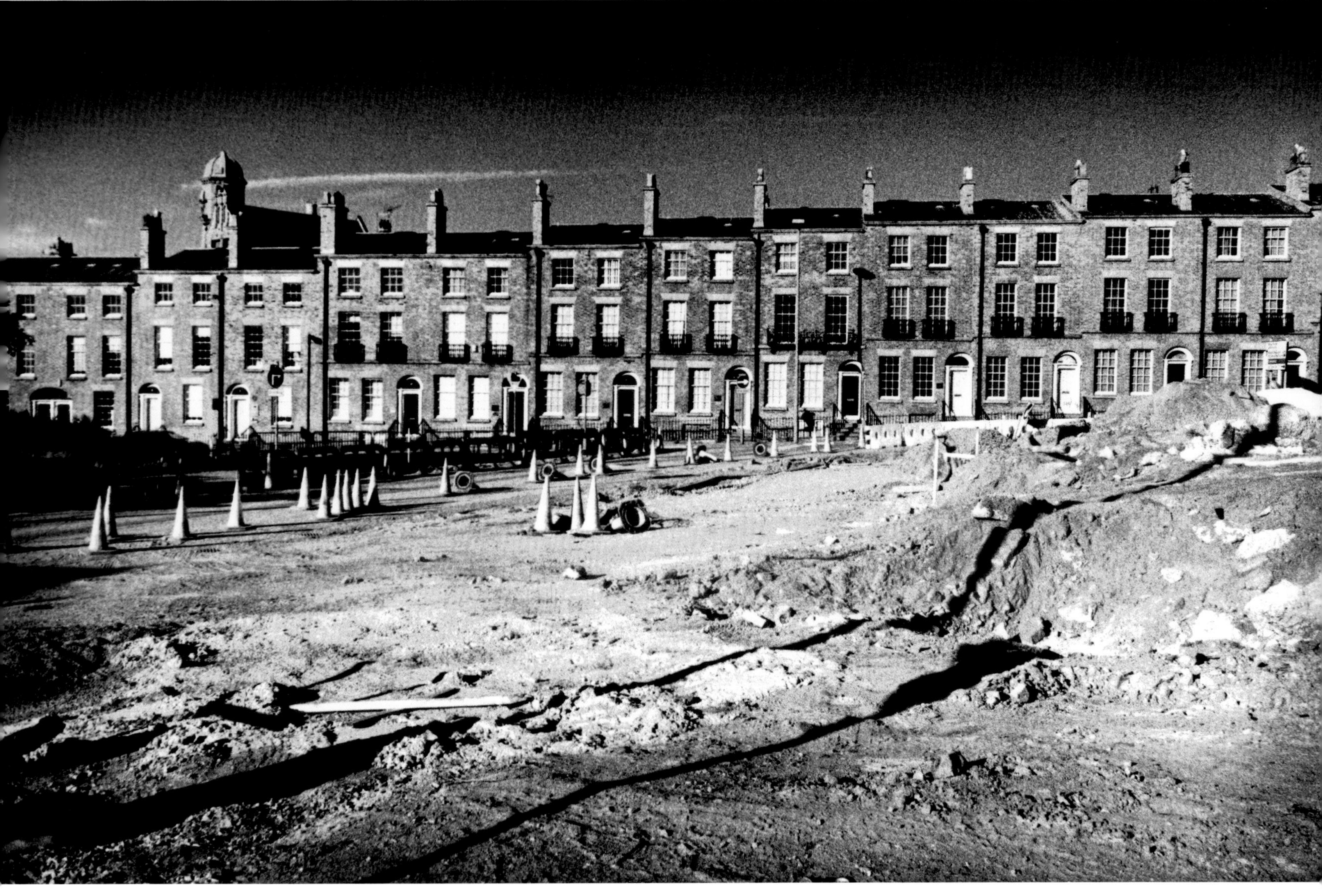

JULY 2005

Seymour Terrace, Seymour Street, c.1810, probably by John Foster Senior, restored 1992

No longer houses but offices for charities, solicitors and the like, this is nevertheless a terrace that still defines what it was to live a life of gentle repose on the upper slopes of Liverpool in the early nineteenth century. The regular, pleasing rhythm of the terrace as it rises up the street acts as a steady rebuke to the disorder of the roadworks in front. Here is a sense of proportion, a stately progress that defies the change all around.

FEBRUARY 2007

St Andrew's Gardens,
John Hughes for Liverpool Corporation Housing Department, 1932–35

This is the archway that carries a transformed St Andrew's Street through a new urban landscape, designed in the 1930s as the venue for a new way of living in the centre of the city. Here, the road is no longer a mere conduit between the crowded and cramped dwellings of the poor, it is an axial avenue between and right through five-storey blocks that came complete will all modern conveniences and the invaluable amenities of space and light. Sun balconies, power points and gas copper boilers were the symbols of a cleaner way of life several feet off the ground. The Director of Housing in Liverpool at the time, Lancelot Keay, saw a future for the city centre as a place to live. The end of insanitary slums need not mean the end of life at the heart of things. The difference would be in how space was arranged; small and irregular streets were to give way to large plots where rationally conceived blocks could rise, while multi-storey dwellings would release space on the ground for broad avenues, parkland and playgrounds.

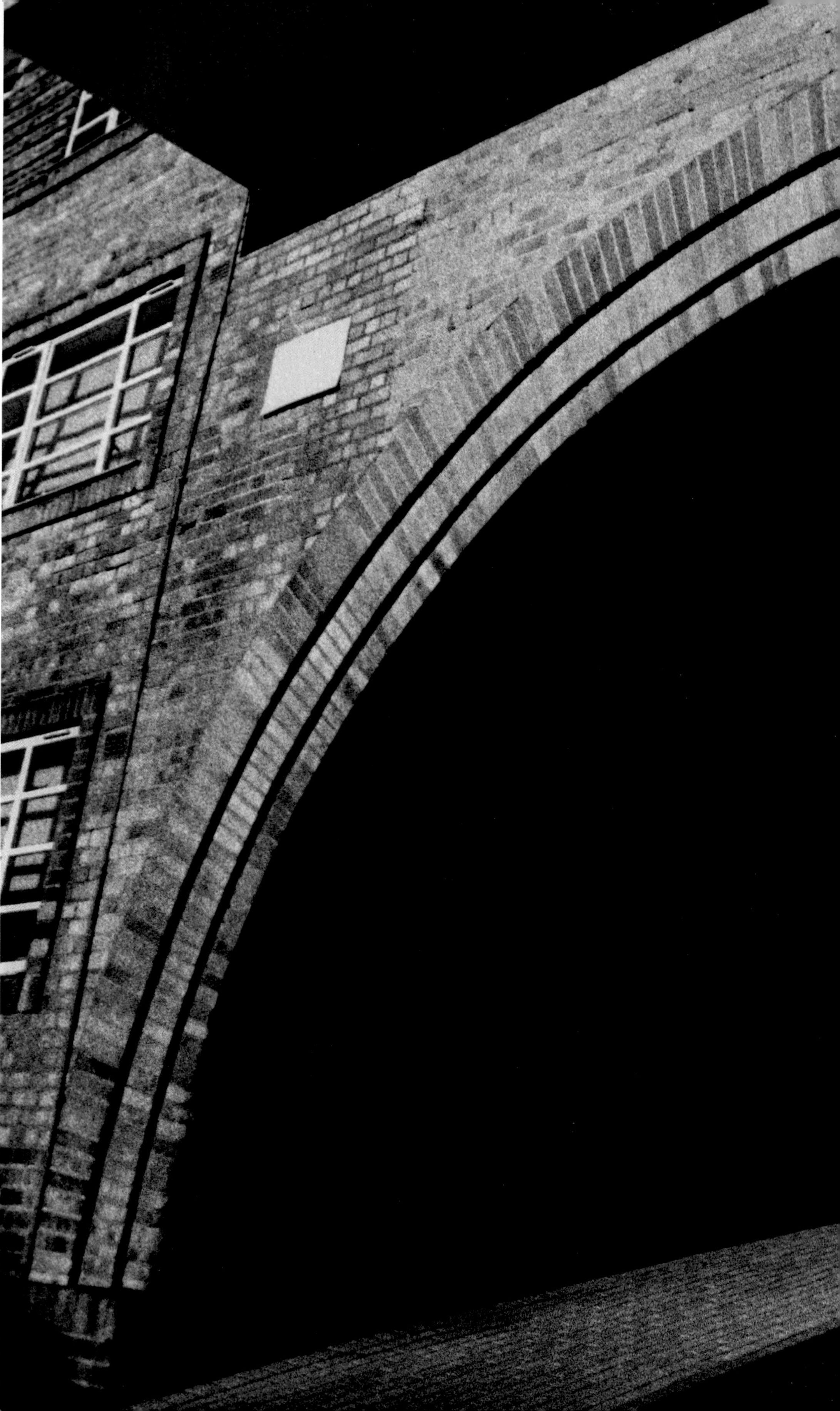

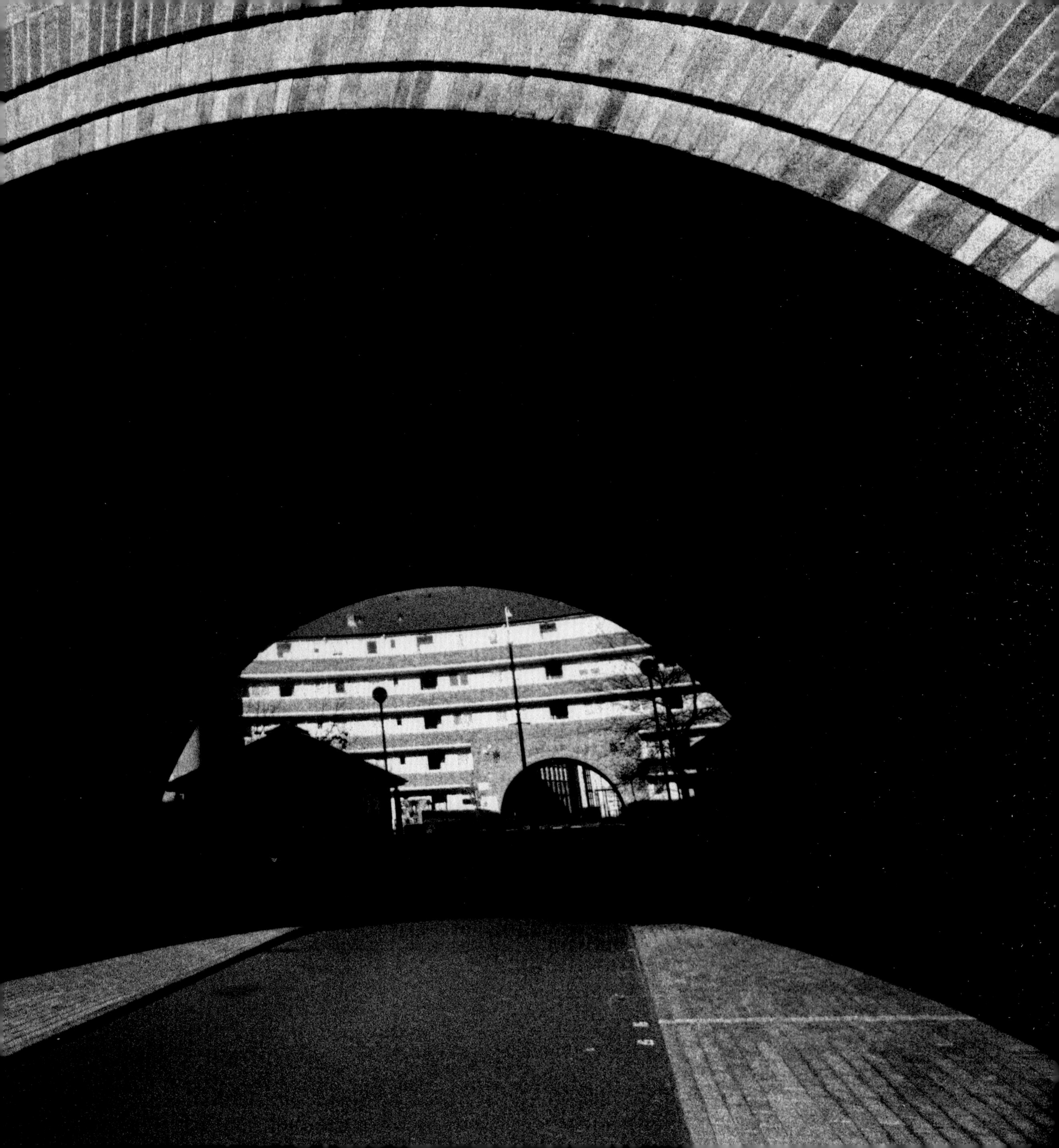

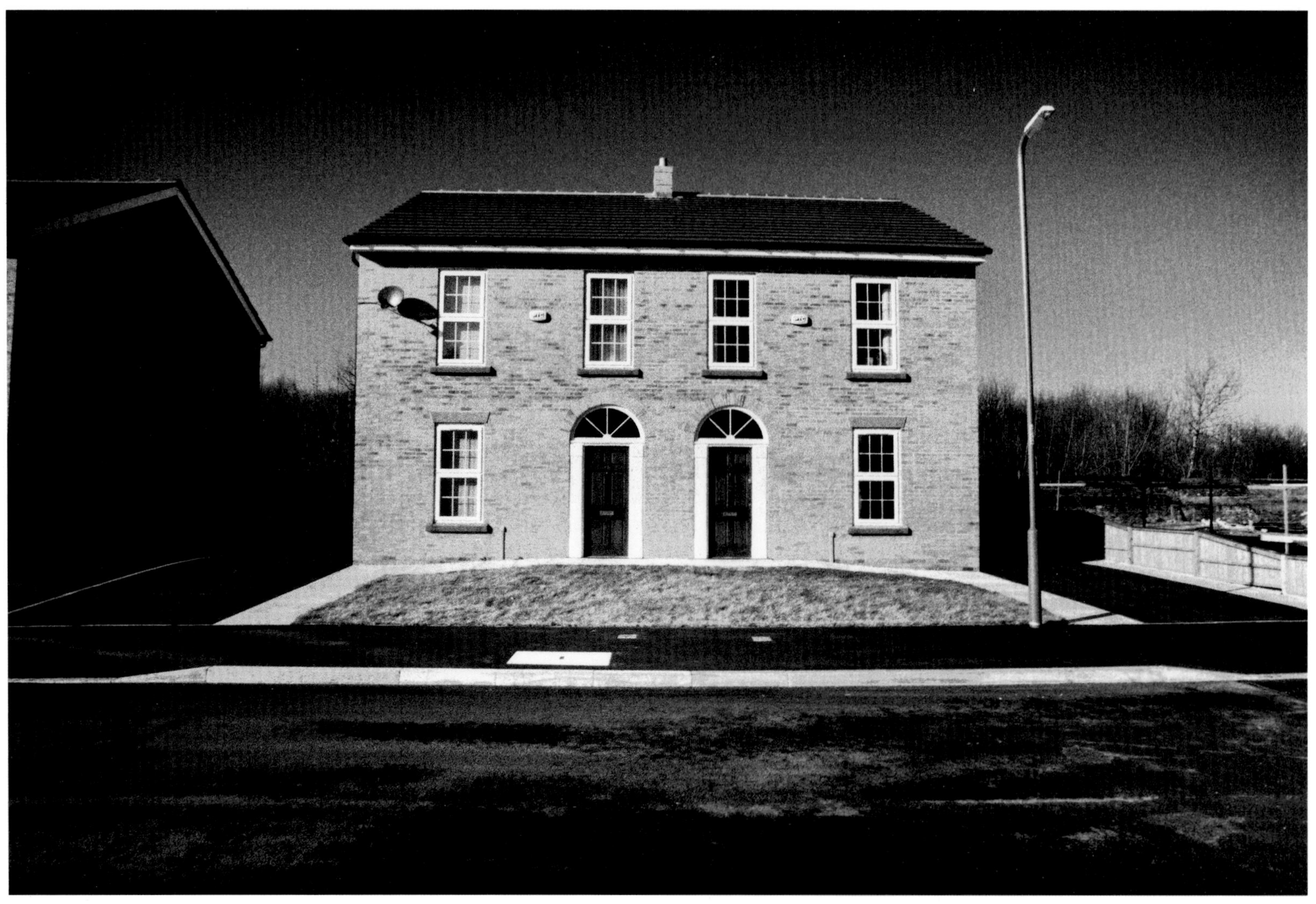

FEBRUARY 2007

Housing on the site of Walton Hospital

As the hospital has scaled back its operations over the years, room has been found for new homes like this. As though assembled from a kit of perfectly formed parts, they sit in their sea of asphalt, looking as though they may belong to another place.

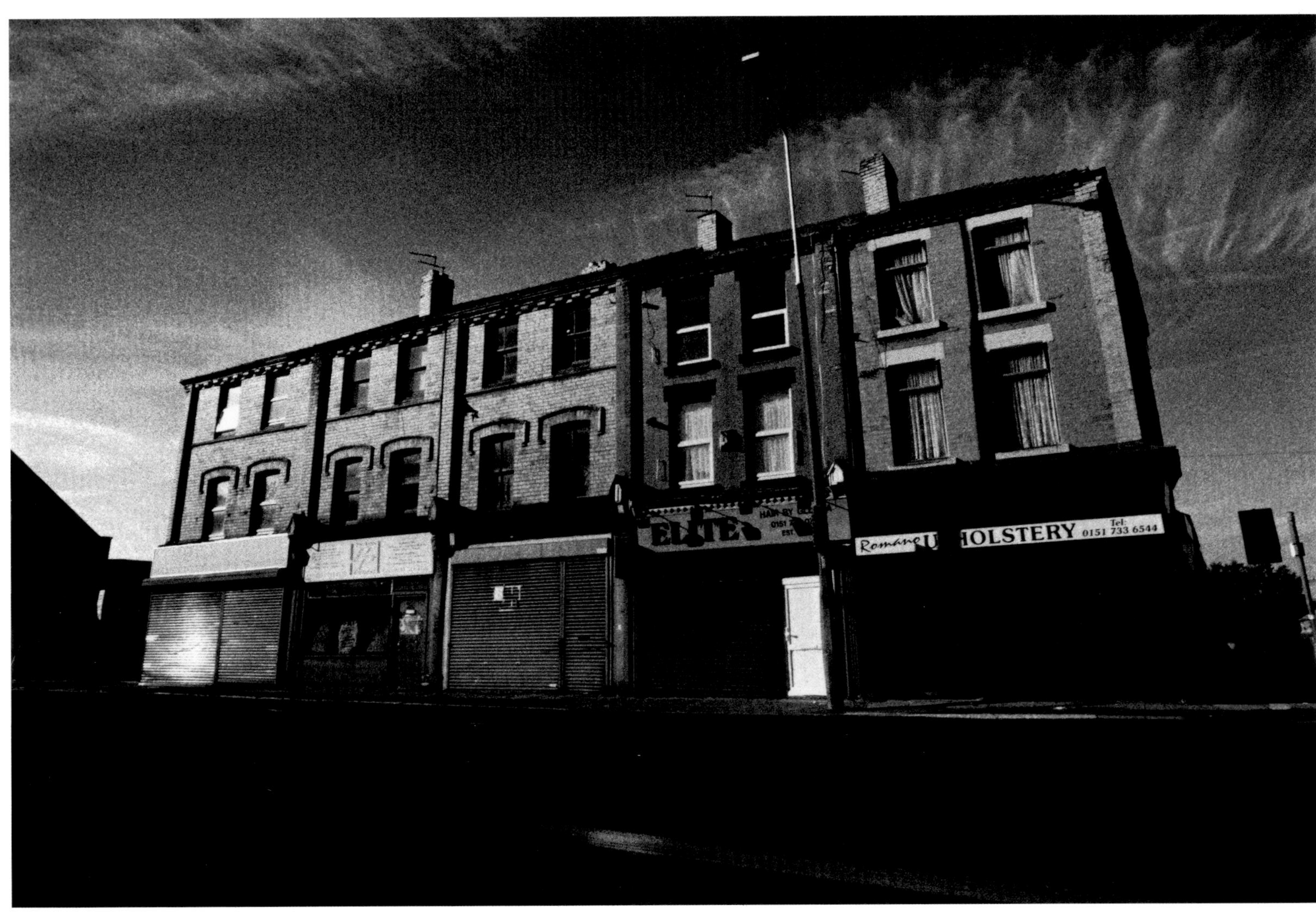

JULY 2007

Shops and housing on Picton Road.

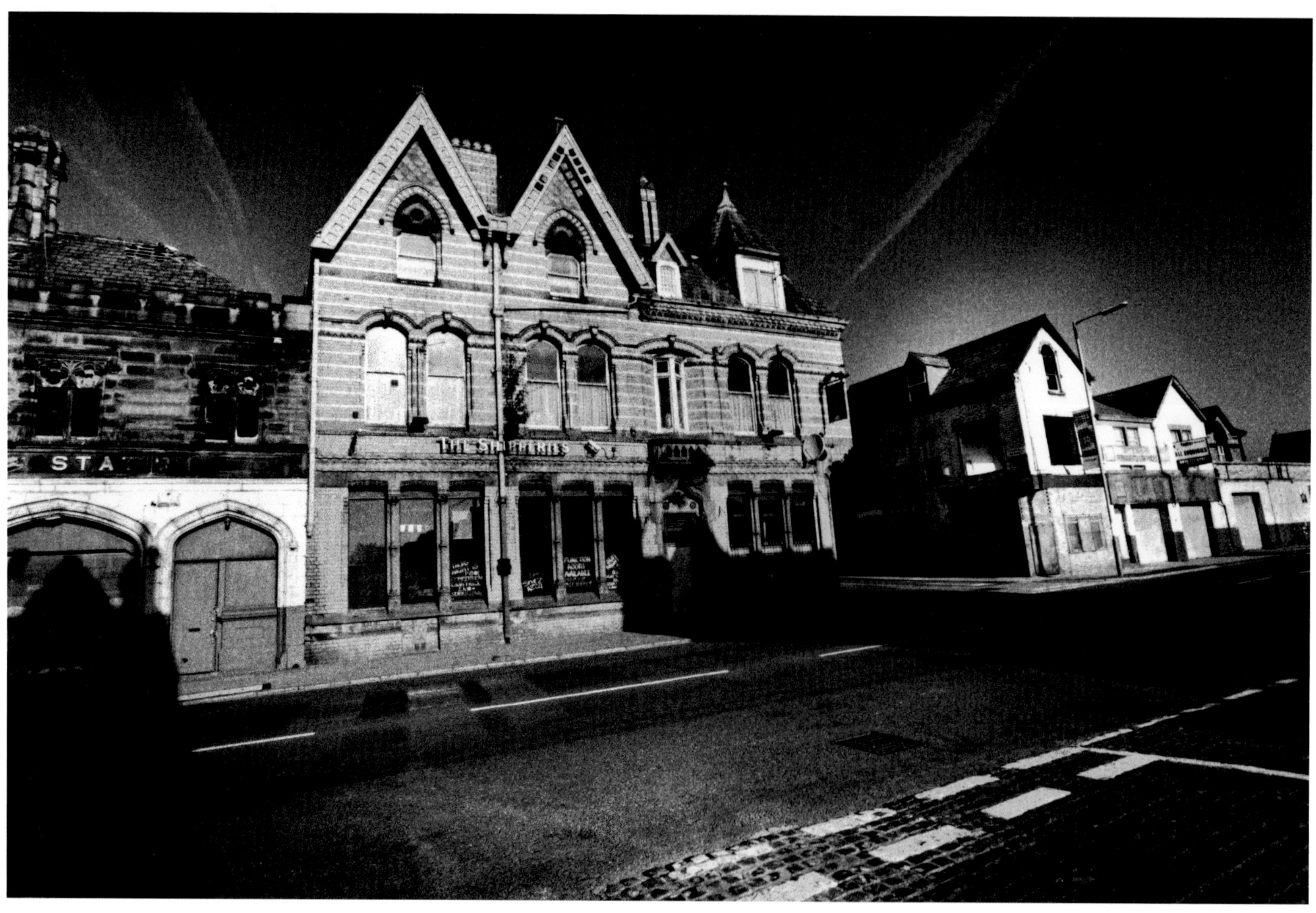

JULY 2006

Buildings on Durning Road, Edge Hill. Far left: police and fire station, mid-nineteenth century

Gothic in a number of guises, this is a Victorian streetscape that typifies the ill-maintained grandeur to be found in a high concentration across so many of the city's inner suburbs. Fire station and shop, pub and houses all lie in their place on the gridiron streets, all with their relationships clearly set and easy to understand, all with their stylistic pretensions and an overwhelming sense of propriety. Edge Hill must find a way to make sense of these buildings and streets again: in a rapidly ageing and unfashionable district it may not be long before gentle decline gives way to grandiose, inferior visions of an alternative future.

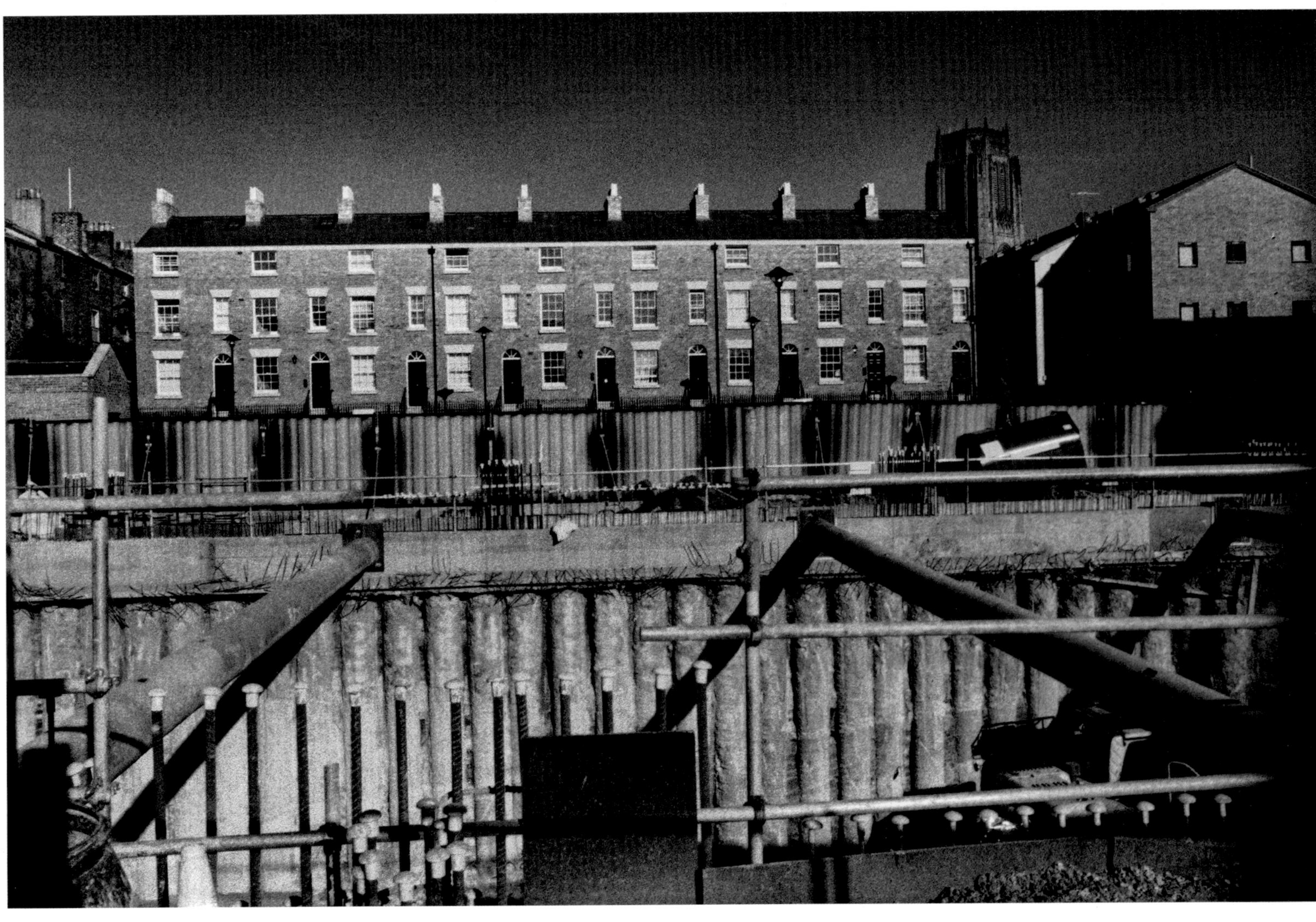

JUNE 2006

Former back-to-back dwellings, off Duke Street, built between 1836 and 1848, restored for Maritime Housing Association by Wilkinson Hindle Halsall Lloyd, completed 2003

Cleaning, re-pointing and a wash of light are distortions to the history of these houses. These are the only remaining back-to-back houses in a city that made a speciality of moulding living accommodation from the most implausible of arrangements, from cellars, courts and buildings with only one side of windows.

The central spine wall of this terrace has long since been breached, long before its most recent restoration, making half the number of houses from the same space but with twice the number of windows. Now they stand fully formed, their exposition to the street by means of the gradual thinning of surrounding buildings offering them the illusion of normality. Only histories and the spread of knowledge will keep alive what they were, and what they tell us about the way in which some Liverpudlians used to live.

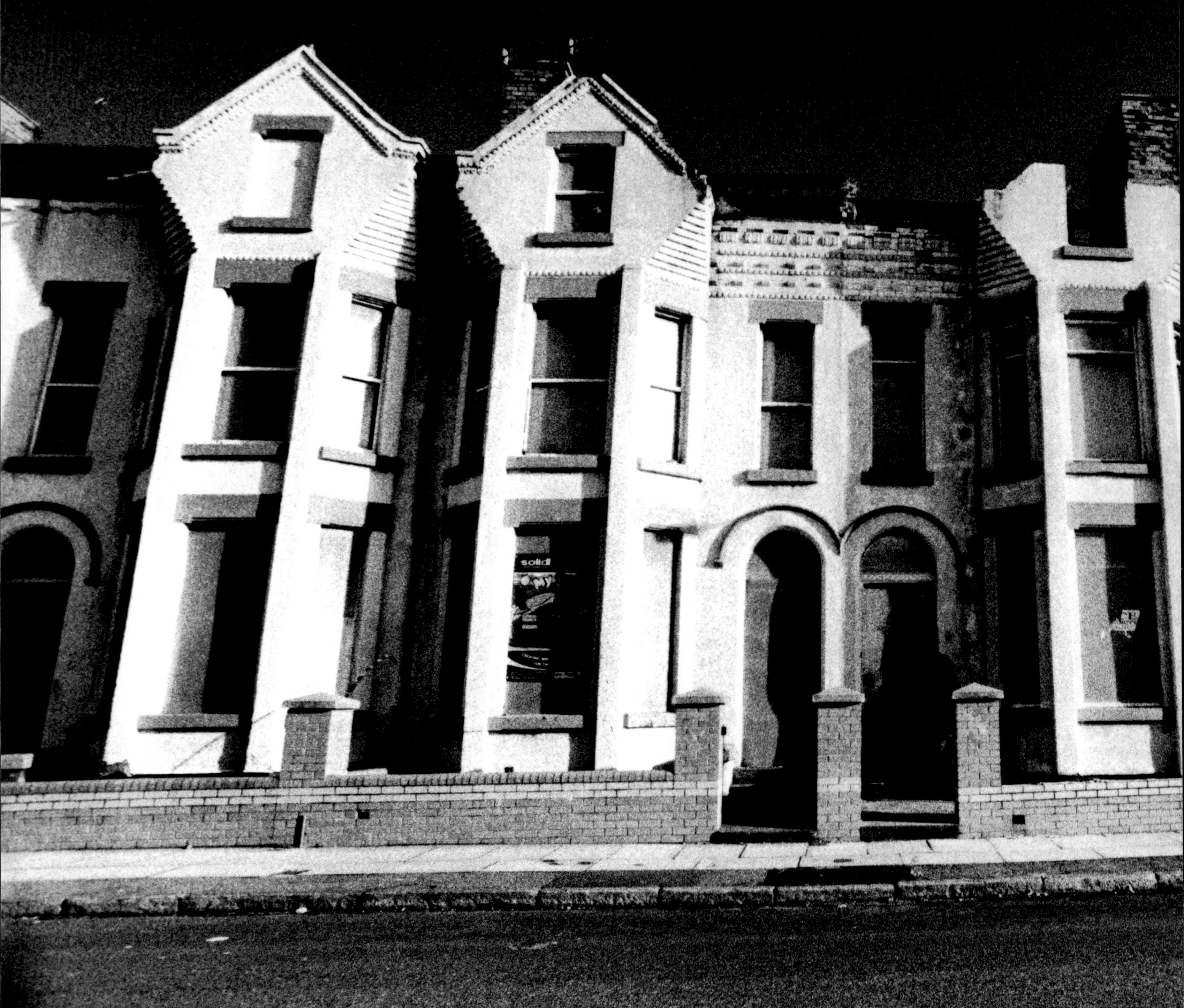
solid!

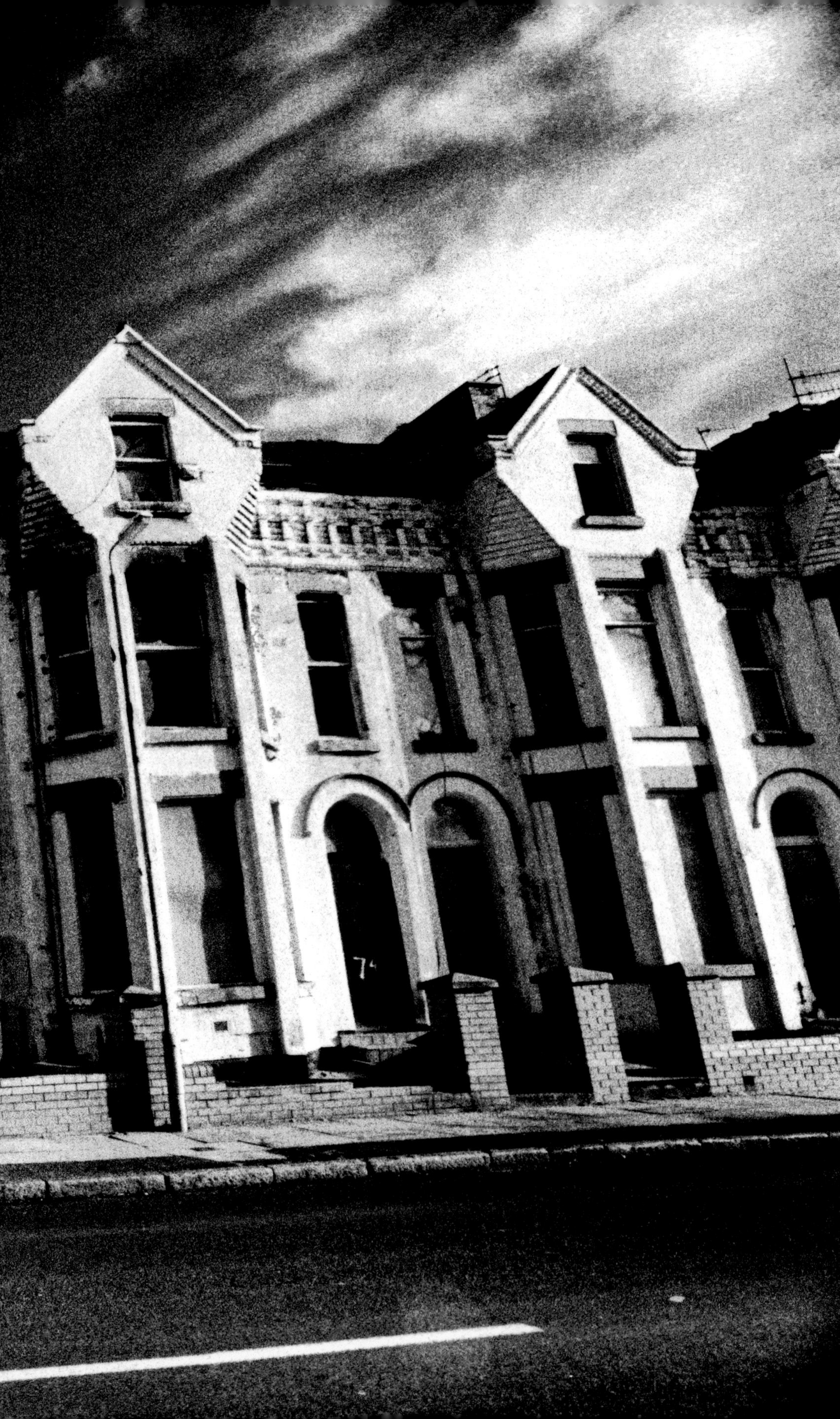

JANUARY 2007

Houses on Hertford Road, Bootle

These homes have now been demolished, to be replaced with new social housing under the terms of the New Heartlands scheme directed by central government. Still standing proudly in the sun, their whitewashed brick and extraordinary lozenge-shaped gables represent a memory of a street now gone and a type of housing now under threat. Across Liverpool, and in its greater urban area such as here in Bootle, houses with both solidity and verve have failed to find a sustainable future, their optimistic and well-intentioned nineteenth-century roots not deep enough to cope with the changed economic circumstances that de-industrialisation has brought.

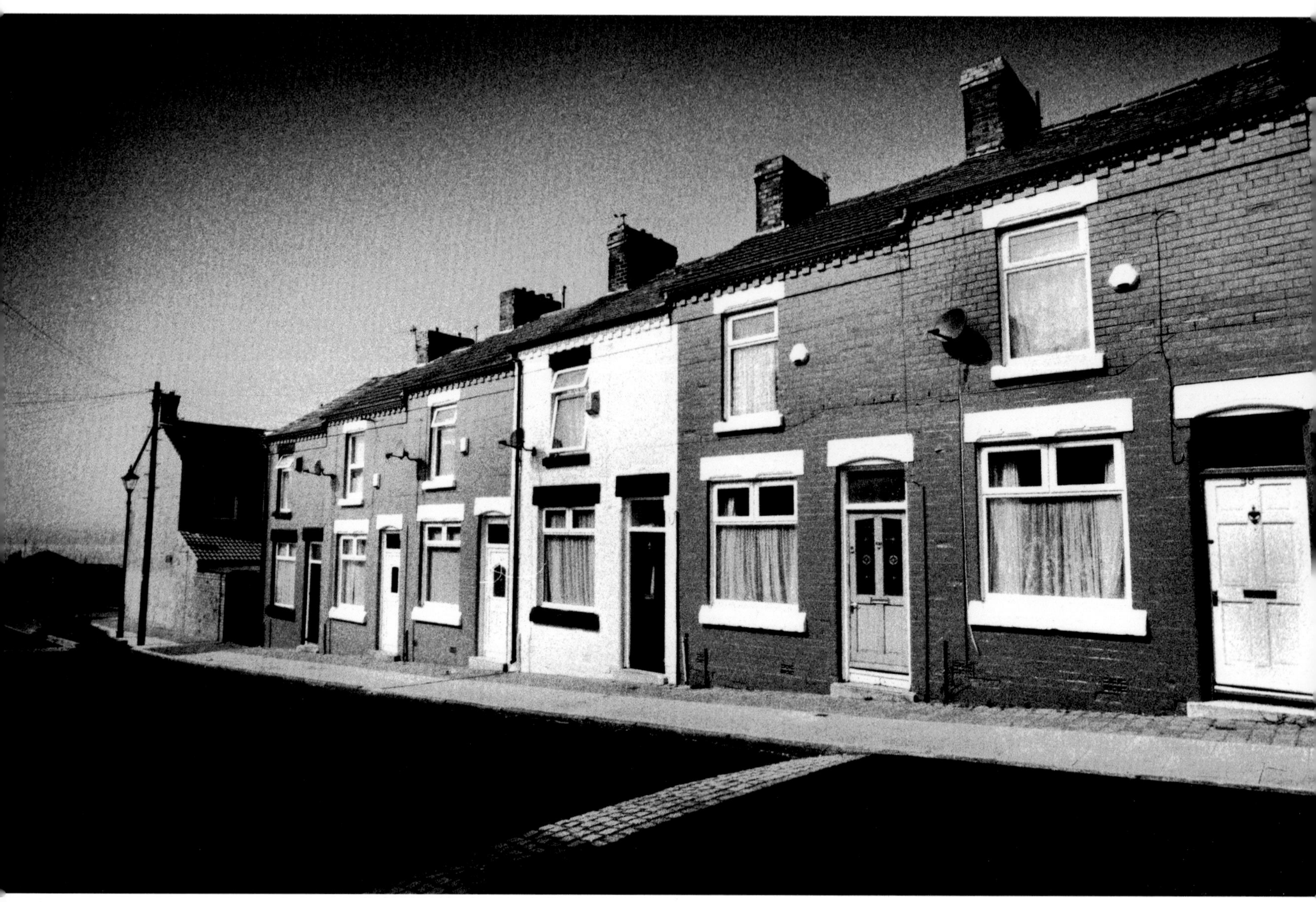

APRIL 2007

Liverpool's urban vernacular, the small red-brick terrace, in its most striking situation. Perched above the Mersey, the Dingle offers an added dimension of drama to houses that play such an important role in the daily life of the city.

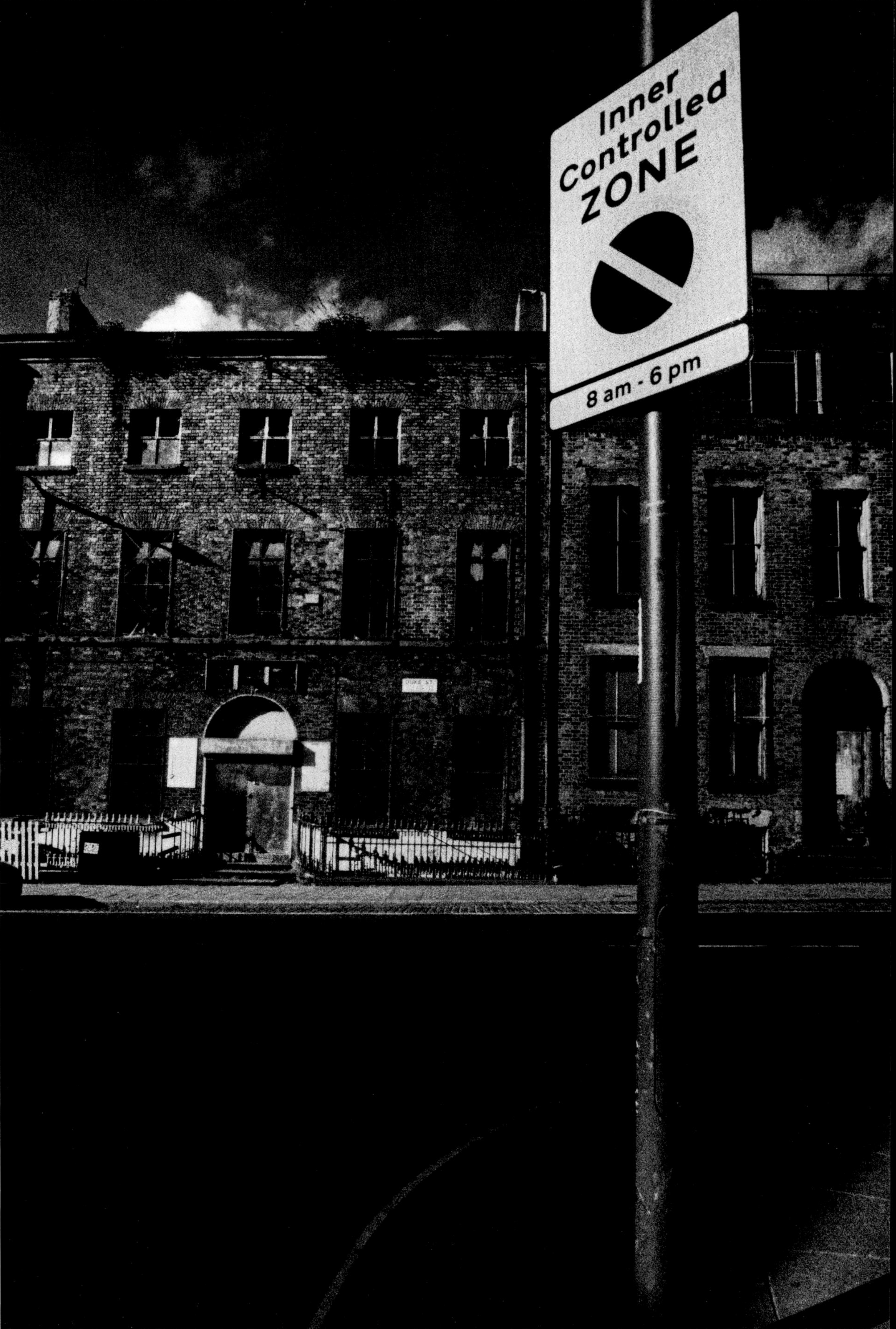

APRIL 2005

Duke Street's eighteenth-century spectacle is just visible through the haze of dirt and decline here. Houses of this quality, in the heart of the city, remain untouched after a flurry of investment all about them.

Ropewalks

Along these straight, long streets can be found the romance of decline mingled in subtle blend with the romance of hope. The buildings here are the houses and warehouses, bars and restaurants, workshops and outlets of more than 200 years of change. They are the tall, narrow buildings of brick, stone and iron of the late eighteenth century, commercial skyscrapers of Liverpool's Enlightenment. They are the houses of genteel repose with the additional shops, counting houses, workshops and storage required of the merchant class; classical proportion and propriety to clothe the everyday matters of trade. They are the taller, tougher warehouses of the nineteenth century. They are the digitally rendered steel, neon and glass of twenty-first-century change. What these buildings are, over and above their actual function, is so much dressing for the streets that carry them down, straightly and elegantly, to Hanover Street and the site of Liverpool's Hanoverian boom. These streets, following the field boundaries that once marked the agricultural territory at the edge of the early eighteenth-century town, stretch in long fingers of parallel rigidity away from the site of the 1715 Old Dock, forming a streetscape of noble practicality. The needs of the dockside were serviced along these thoroughfares, and effectively so, but using a language that said something of the civilised achievement of the commercially successful town. The storage and sale of goods was accommodated here, and the dock-related manufacture of items such as rope, for which the length and straightness of a street was a prerequisite. Housing for all classes was here, too, from the refined perambulations of Duke Street to the court dwellings and back-to-back housing that squeezed, tendril-like, into whatever space was available. All of this, bound up in a regular network of streets that spoke of the excitement and achievement of the early period of modern international trade.

Fortunes are made and lost, hope gives way to reality, and in turn to decline. By the 1980s, dereliction was complete and there was little, if any, sense of that same excitement and achievement. Henry Street, Seel Street and the other ropewalks so close to the very centre of the city were permitted to fall apart into a stupor of abandonment. This was not necessarily complete collapse, except in the case of a few individual buildings, but instead it was the startling phenomenon of decay en masse, as if the aftermath of a war or natural disaster had driven away the sense of the place. The reasons for this are easy enough to ascertain; with the changing spatial arrangement of port-related activity to the north of the centre, and with the eventual long-term decline of these sort of activities altogether, no new, larger purpose was found for these streets. All forms of economic activity became increasingly rare, while some new twentieth-century uses for these buildings, such as nightclubs, added to a sense of tumbledown romance.

Dancing in an eighteenth-century brick-vaulted produce cellar in a building on a street that was once something so integral to the physical economy of Liverpool has a peculiar sort of resonance to it. During the bleakest days (and nights) of decline, there must almost have been a sense that, in these streets with their war-torn appearance, a revolutionary mob had taken over the buildings as part of an armed uprising. Certainly, the sense of rebellion and experimentation implicit in various forms of popular music found an outlet here. Dancing and music are entirely appropriate responses to what happened here architecturally. To dare to build a network of world trade, to create this wealth and these connections; to do all of that and see the forces of pragmatism and the stony-faced logic of the market clear it all away: this demands a reaction. These streets are the memorial to everything that was dismissed so absolutely by the ambitions of other parts of the capitalist world, the same brand of ambition that had created them in the first instance. There is a sublimity in all of this that is done justice by the music and movement of the new activity, and somehow celebrated in it.

In the regeneration of Ropewalks during the last decade, the overriding vision has been that some of the intrinsic nobility of these buildings can be reclaimed (as opposed to the improvised nobility of art merely grafted onto decline). In returning to the view that these streets are an integral part of the city, there is a partial reversal of the notion, ongoing since the 1830s, that civility and dignity in the urban form of Liverpool can only be found 'up the hill', on the grid plan of the early nineteenth-century district lying between Abercromby Square and Falkner Square, or beyond to the serpentine avenues of Princes and Sefton parks. The exodus of residents from these streets towards the latest version of fashionable living began a very long time ago, but now the restrained classicism of the remaining eighteenth-century houses is enjoying a renewed enthusiasm; restoration of the old and an echoing of this residential aesthetic in the new is now commonplace. Where brand new buildings are inserted into this historic streetscape, an uncluttered style is typically employed, picking and mixing from various of the modernist ideas active during the last seventy years. This, of course, is a natural fit with the rationalism of the eighteenth- and early nineteenth-century streetscape. Gradually, with every building restoration, re-filling of gaps and the evolution of function, this has become a part of the city that seems vital and important.

Far from experiencing a heightened, smooth-surfaced gentrification, Ropewalks wears its rough edges with pride. Just a decade or so since regeneration money started flowing into the area, there can be no doubt that there is much work left to do, but the current mixture of gloss and disrepair lends the place an atmosphere of continuing possibility, of creativity and success yet to come. This selection of photographs concentrates on the process of renewal in Ropewalks captured at a certain moment in time, and the sites of decline viewed before hope is even detectable. There is no overwhelming sense, from these images, of the success stories and the completed renewal. Instead, this is Ropewalks in a raw state, the way it must be read and understood. Trade, warehousing and the like have all come and gone, and new functions come to replace them, but what remains constant is the brick, and the height and the straightness of the streets. These photographs capture a sense of these constants in a site of rapid change.

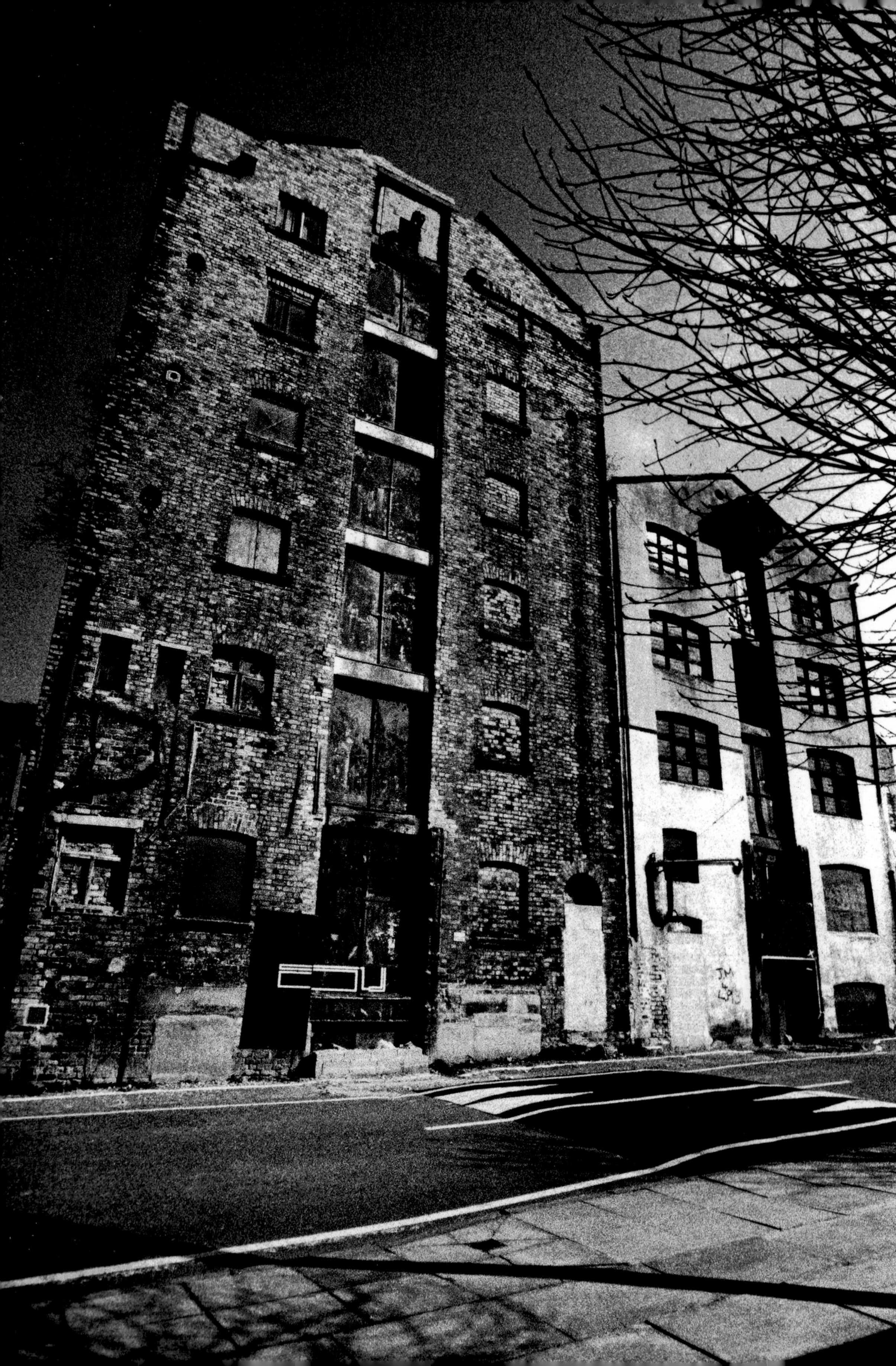

MARCH 2003

Warehousing on Lydia Ann Street

FEBRUARY 2006

Far right: part of 'The Foundry' mixed-use scheme, Maritime Housing Association, under construction.

Lydia Ann Street begins its transformation from brick to steel. A neglected back street has been coaxed back into the city and given a real use once again.

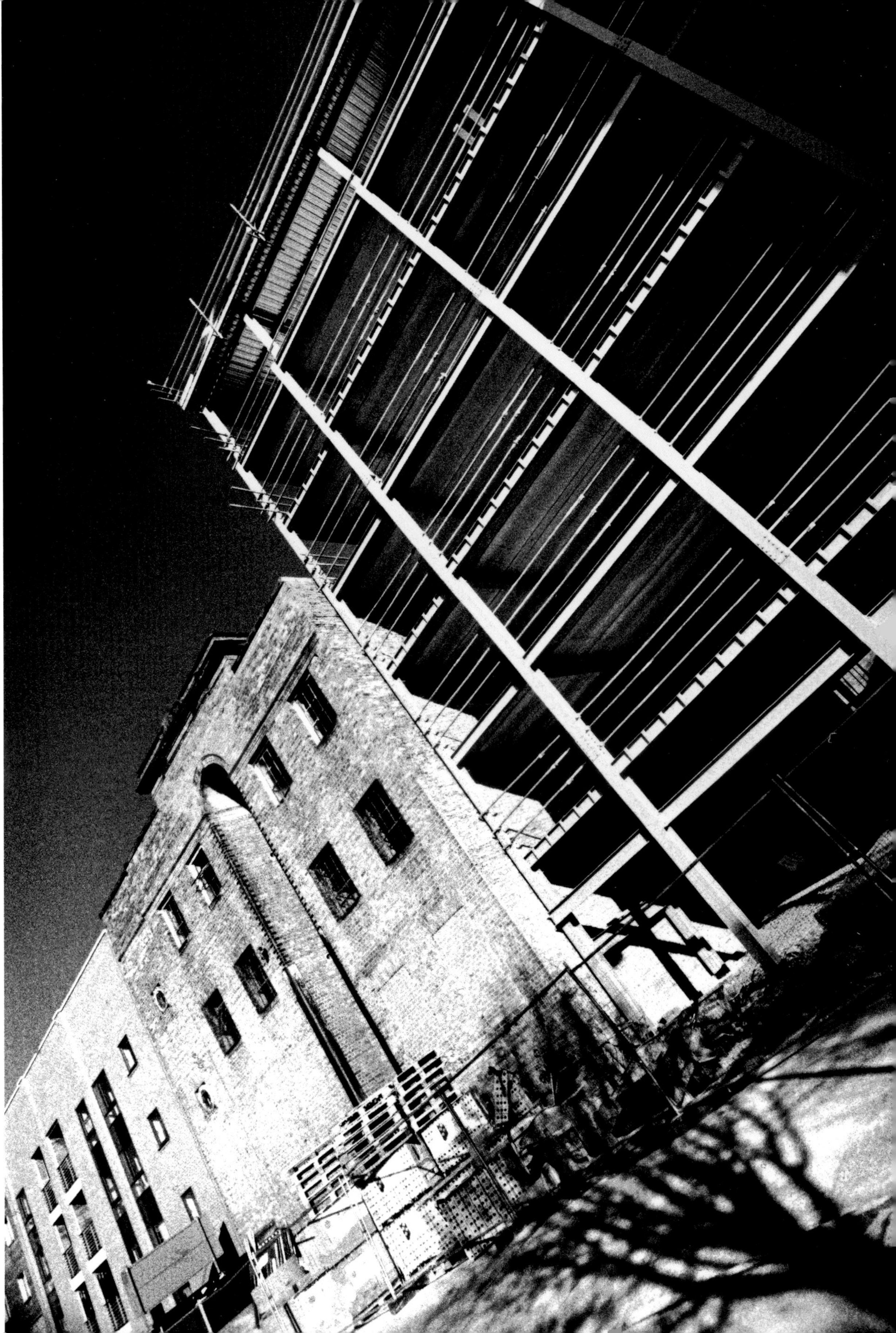

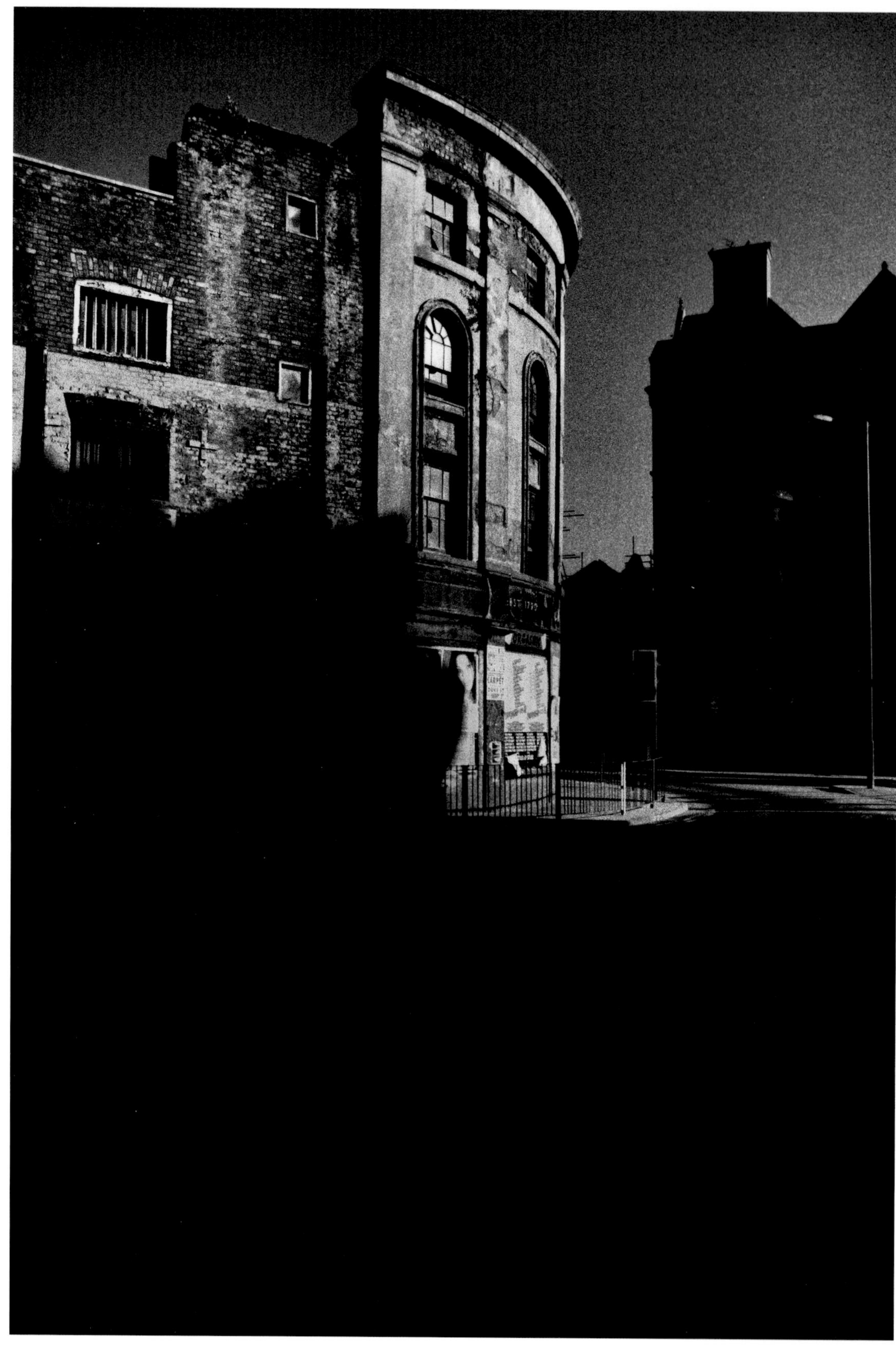

APRIL 2001

Casartelli Building, architects unrecorded, c.1760

Were it not for the visual clues such as the traffic lights and safety barriers, this view of the Casartelli building on the corner of Hanover Street and Duke Street would seem to exist outside any particular time, capturing a building in steep physical decline among the gathering gloom. In fact, following a partial collapse of this structure in October 2000, this photograph stands as something of a memorial to a significant piece of Liverpool's history now lost forever. Restoration of the building was deemed to be impractical due to the nature and extent of the decay. Since 2006, a glossy replica of this building has stood on the same site, the extraordinary outcome of the debate sparked by the demise of this fine sliver of eighteenth-century Liverpool.

From the mid-nineteenth century to the Great Depression of the 1930s, this building was the home of Anthony Casartelli and Sons, manufacturers of scientific instruments such as microscopes and thermometers. Microscopes, among their many other uses, can be used as linen provers, checking the quality of cloth. Ships require any number of scientific instruments for their smooth running. This was a building and, for most of its life, a business that was at the very heart of Liverpool's economy.

APRIL 2001

A fragment of an eighteenth-century terrace on Duke Street, more like a piece of film set than an actual part of the city. Within four years, this ruinous plot was reintegrated into the real life of Ropewalks, becoming the building shown on p.47.

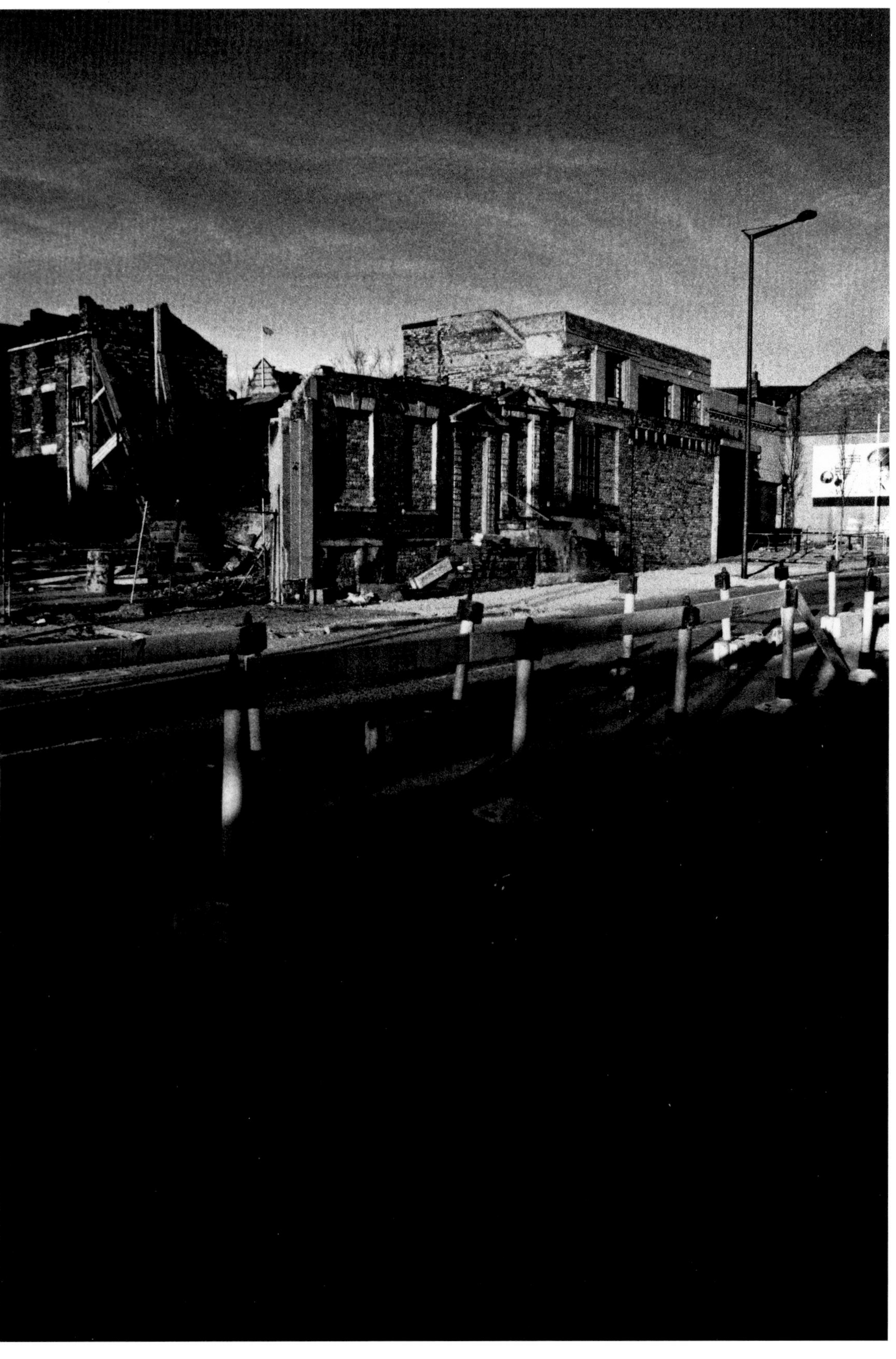

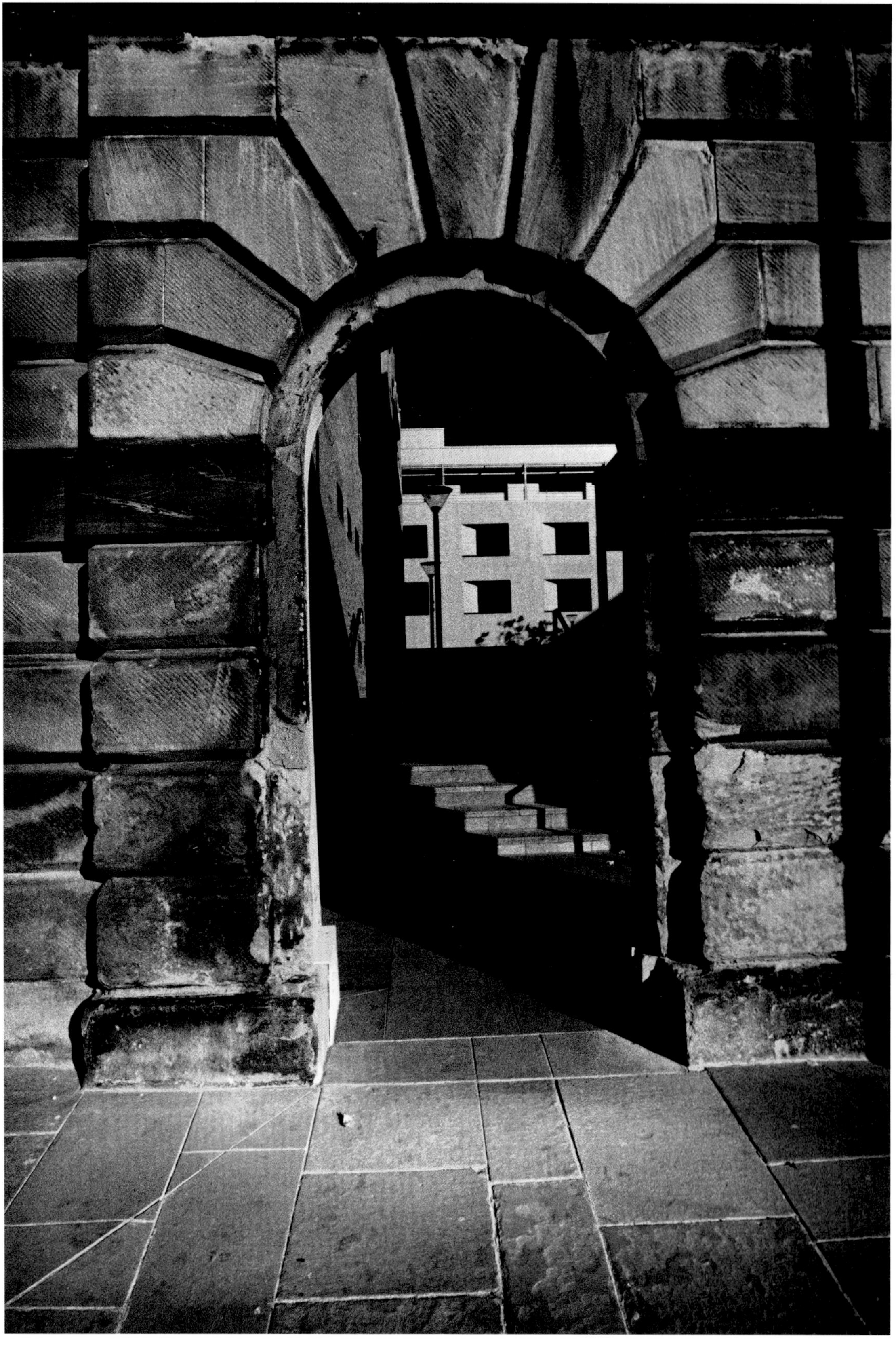

MAY 2005

Foreground: Rusticated masonry wall and arched doorway, the surviving remains of the Kent Street oil mill of Alexander M. Smith & Co.
Through the doorway: 'East Village' apartment development, Madison Square (off Kent Street), Falconer Chester Hall architects, completed 2003

Through a fragment of architecture past lies the promise of a new vitality. Kent Street has risen and fallen through countless different versions of itself. This has been variously the site of merchants' houses, warehousing, municipal buildings, a mill for grinding seed into oil, slum housing and five-storey tenement blocks built by the corporation as part of the slum clearance schemes of the mid-twentieth century. All have come and gone, leaving behind just a few pieces of evidence for their existence and, in exceptional cases, physical remains. One small part of the ground floor wall of the former Liverpool Gas Company has been incorporated by the architects of the new apartment complex, the rusticated masonry leading up to the smooth brick surfaces of the residential blocks. Neither the conservation of the wall nor the architecture of the new buildings are at all remarkable, but together they form an example, typical in Ropewalks, of the utilisation of history in the service of new development.

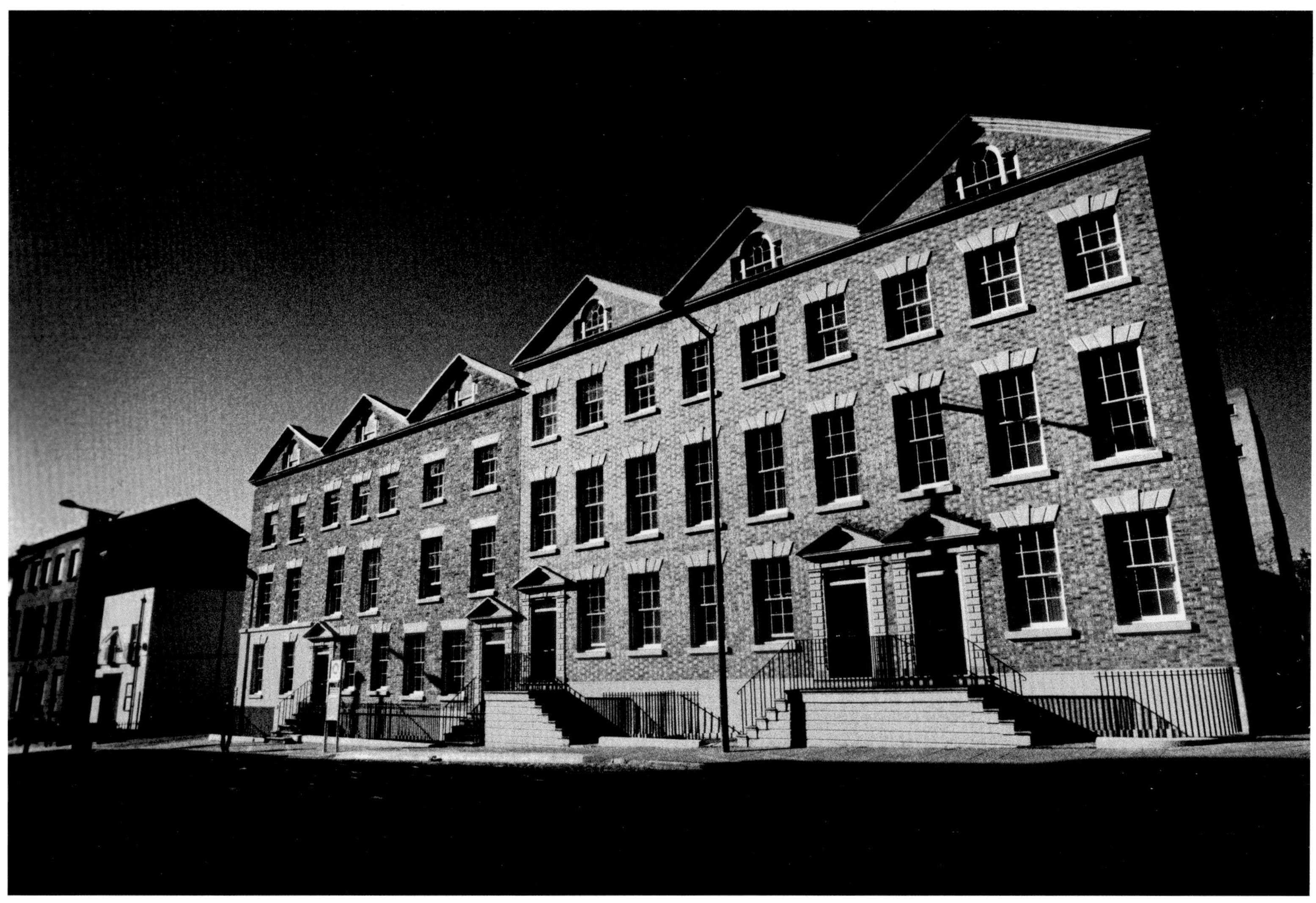

MAY 2005

Housing for Maritime Housing Association, Wilkinson Hindle Halsall Lloyd, completed 2003

Eighteenth-century Duke Street is reborn with a facsimile of the houses left to rot on this site for decades. The stump of a wall containing the two staggered doorways seen in the middle of these two housing ranges was the root from which the entire edifice sprang. Historic recreations have had less to work with than that. Considerable stretches of Duke Street still contain complete but unhappy Georgian houses that have received no maintenance or investment for many years, but the random process of grant-giving was such that this completely ruined site was transmogrified back into existence. It is hard not to be impressed by the power of this act – this gabled rhythm reasserts an important sense of the eighteenth-century streetscape – but as in the case of the Casartelli building, one would prefer that careful maintenance took the place of guilty reproduction.

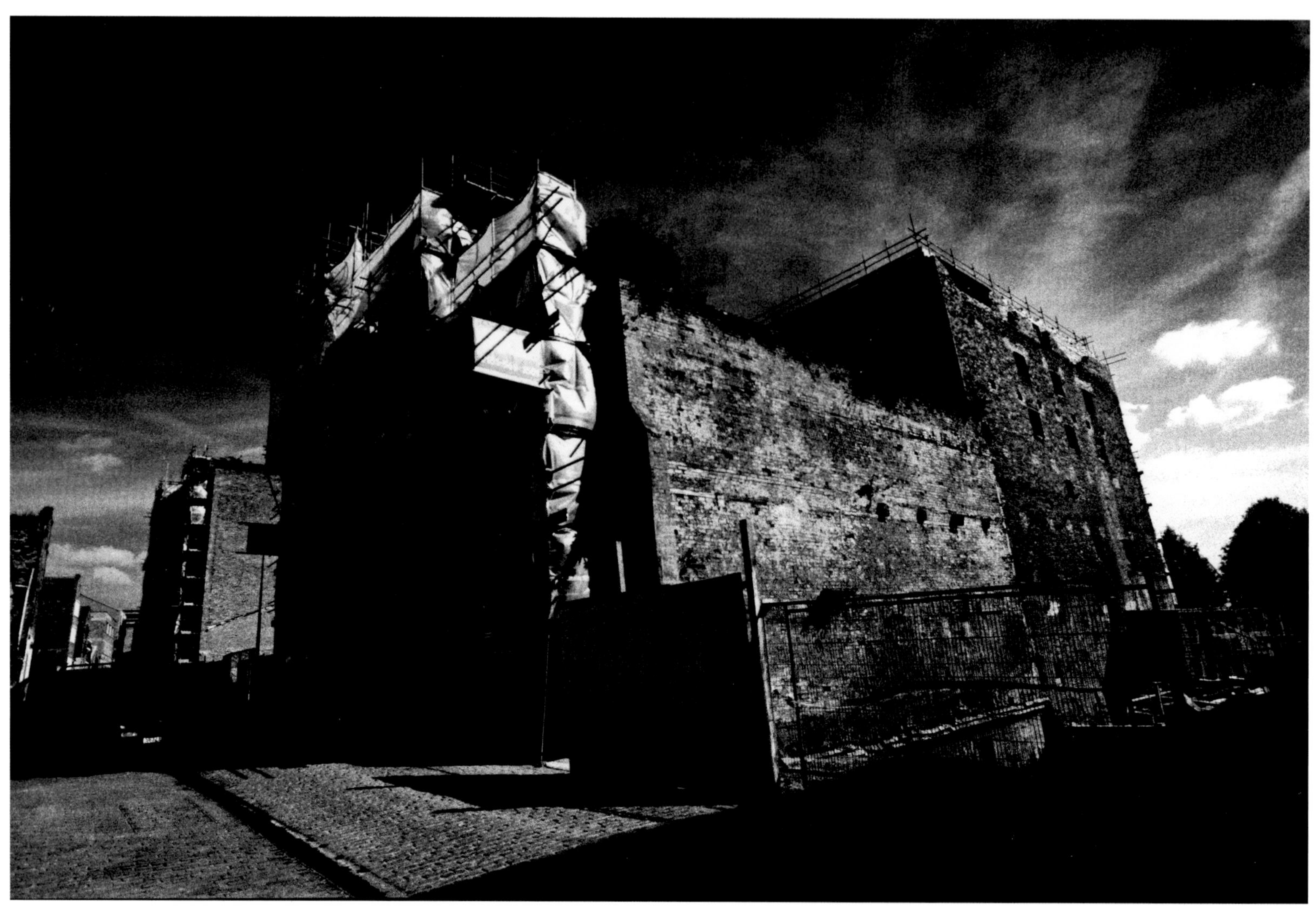

MAY 2005

A block between Henry Street and Lydia Ann Street is prepared for metamorphosis with scaffold and plastic sheeting. The vegetation present across its face suggests that this is remedial action to prevent it from crossing the boundary from architecture into a naturally occurring formation.

AUGUST 2001

Houses in Cleveland Square, various architects, late eighteenth to nineteenth centuries

This is one side of a square that no longer possesses its other three sides. Less of a square and more of a street, the extent of the dilapidation here calls even that description into question. Standing at this point, though, it is still just about possible to imagine the significance of these houses in the urban form of nineteenth-century Liverpool, standing as a nodal point along the line that Frederick Street once took, running parallel to the river towards the original wet dock in the present-day Canning Place. This eighteenth-century square gathered a number of decorative accretions in the nineteenth century and gained a retail function at ground-floor level. In the late twentieth century, the majority of the land on which it stood was used to widen major roads and build low-rise social housing. Now this side of the square, in a belated acknowledgment of historic significance, has been rebuilt behind what was left of the façade of these buildings, their innards reconfigured into the dimensions of modern apartments and their skins preened into the neatness of an imagined nineteenth-century shopping street. An authentic, if crumbling, fragment of what had long passed is now commemorated in a few stray brick courses and stone lintels affixed unconvincingly to a large, steel-framed modern block stretching back to Argyle Street.

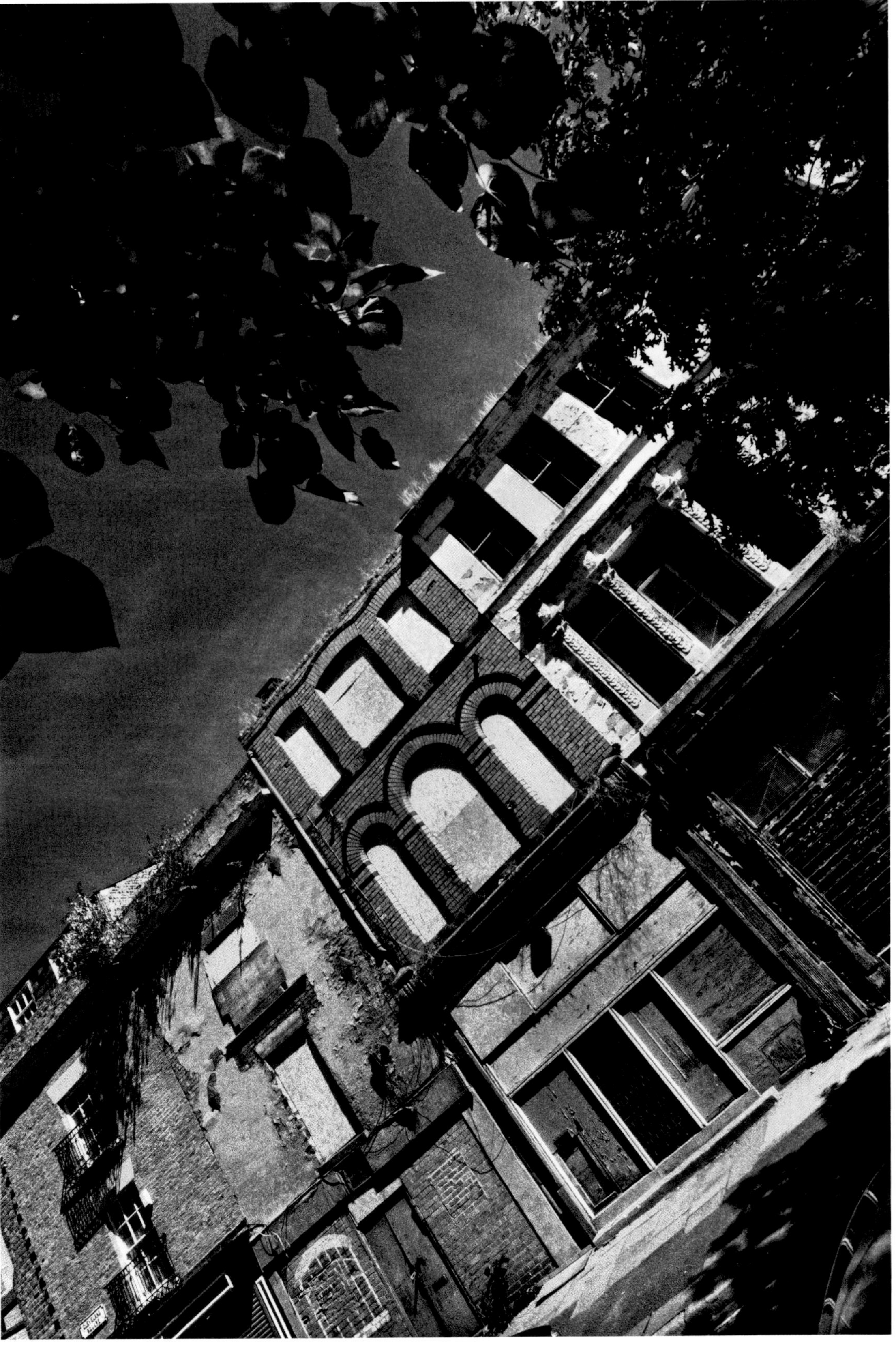

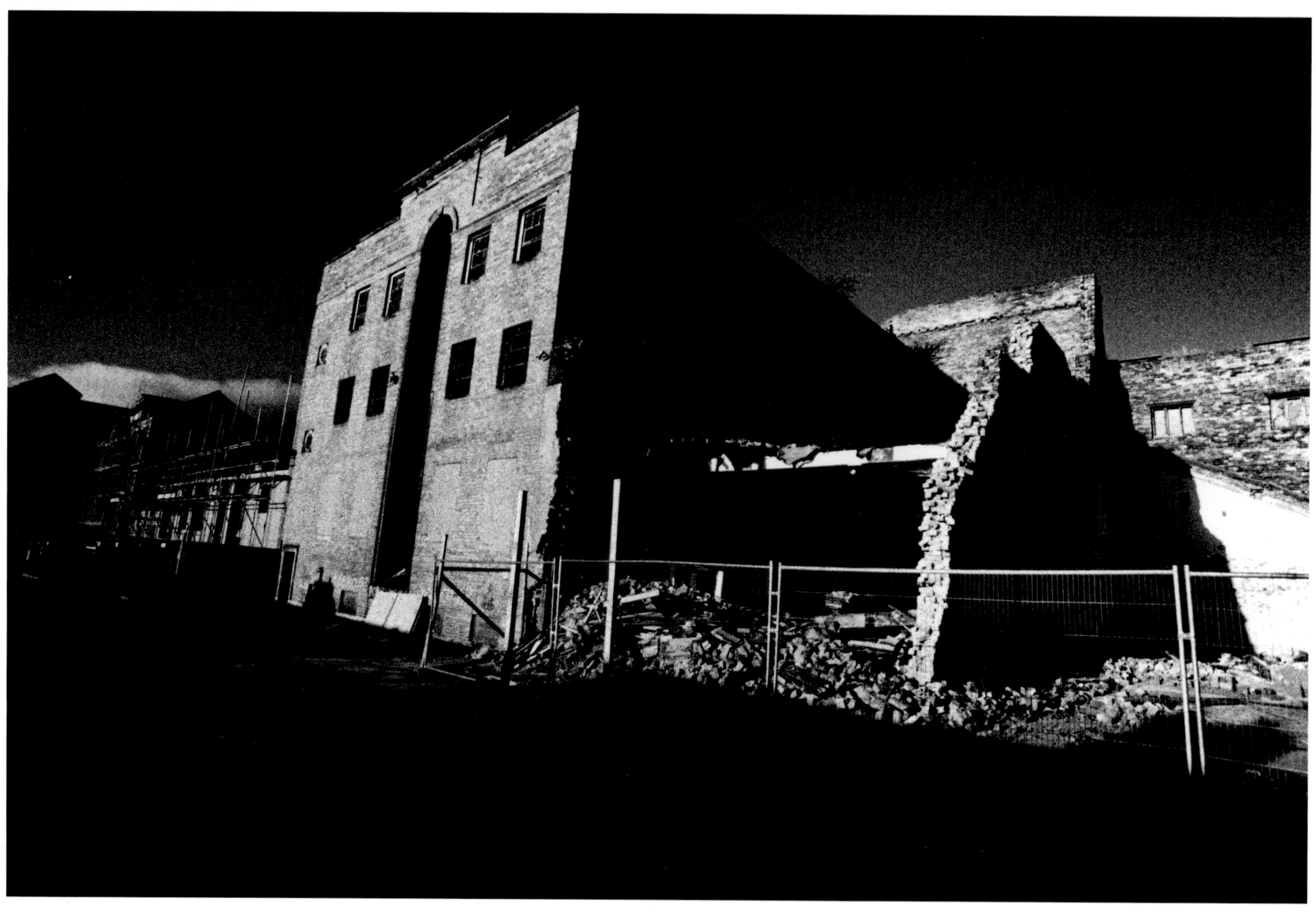

NOVEMBER 2003

Warehouse in Lydia Ann Street, probably 1930s

This squat, muscular warehouse demonstrates a strong continuity of built form along these streets. Even in the mid-twentieth century when the volume of goods coming from the central docks nearest to Lydia Ann Street was in steep decline, an up-to-date version of the same warehouse type that had dominated this area since the late eighteenth century could still be conceived of. The crumbled structure to the right, meanwhile, awaits its redevelopment. Today, the entirety of this side of the street consists of an unbroken chain of apartment blocks, the newly-built abutting the old warehouses that were able to be converted. This example is now book-ended with two modern blocks, losing a sense of its monumentality but gaining a secure future in its new role.

MAY 2005

The 'Cinnamon' Building, on the corner of Suffolk Street and Henry Street

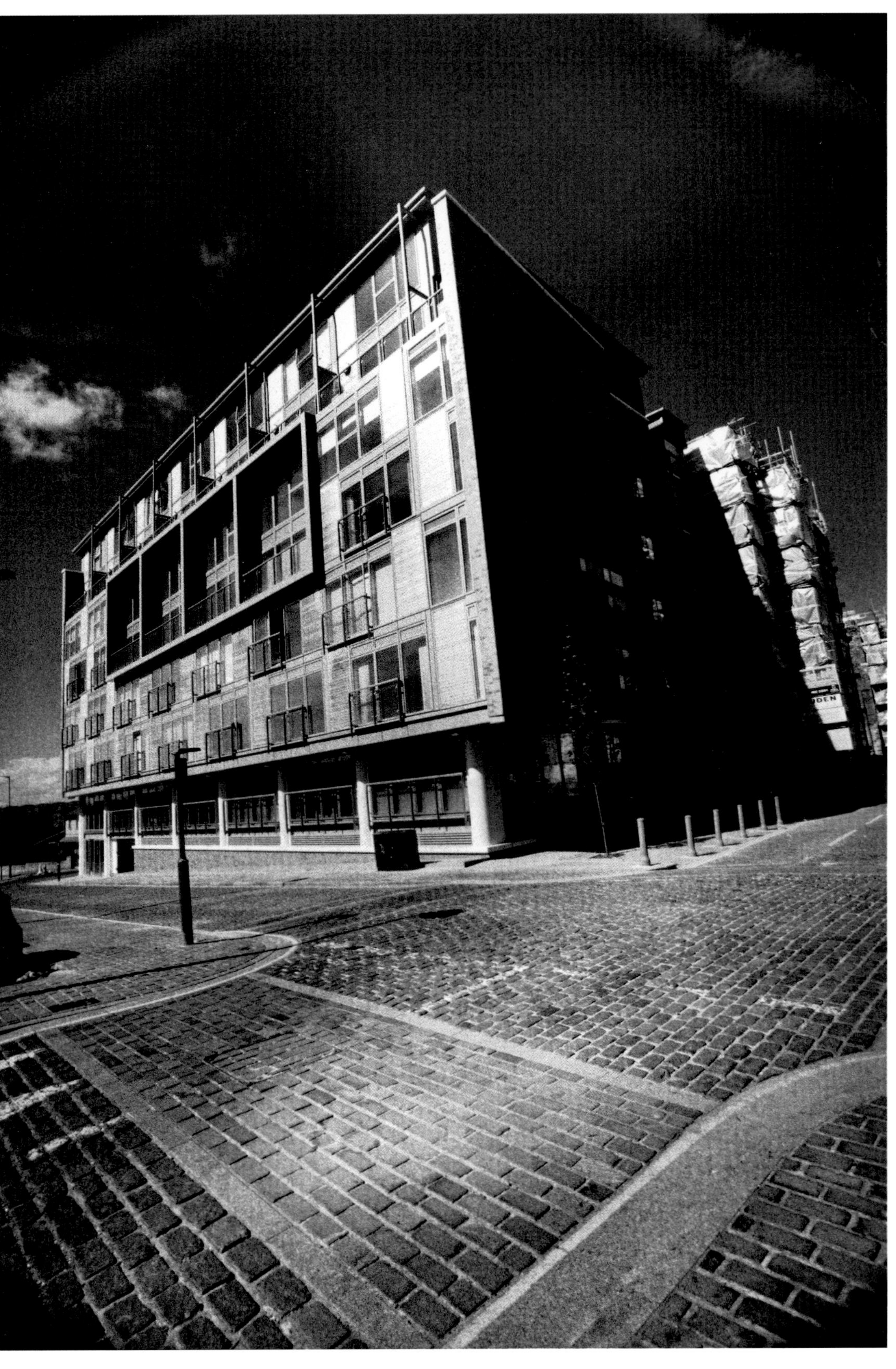

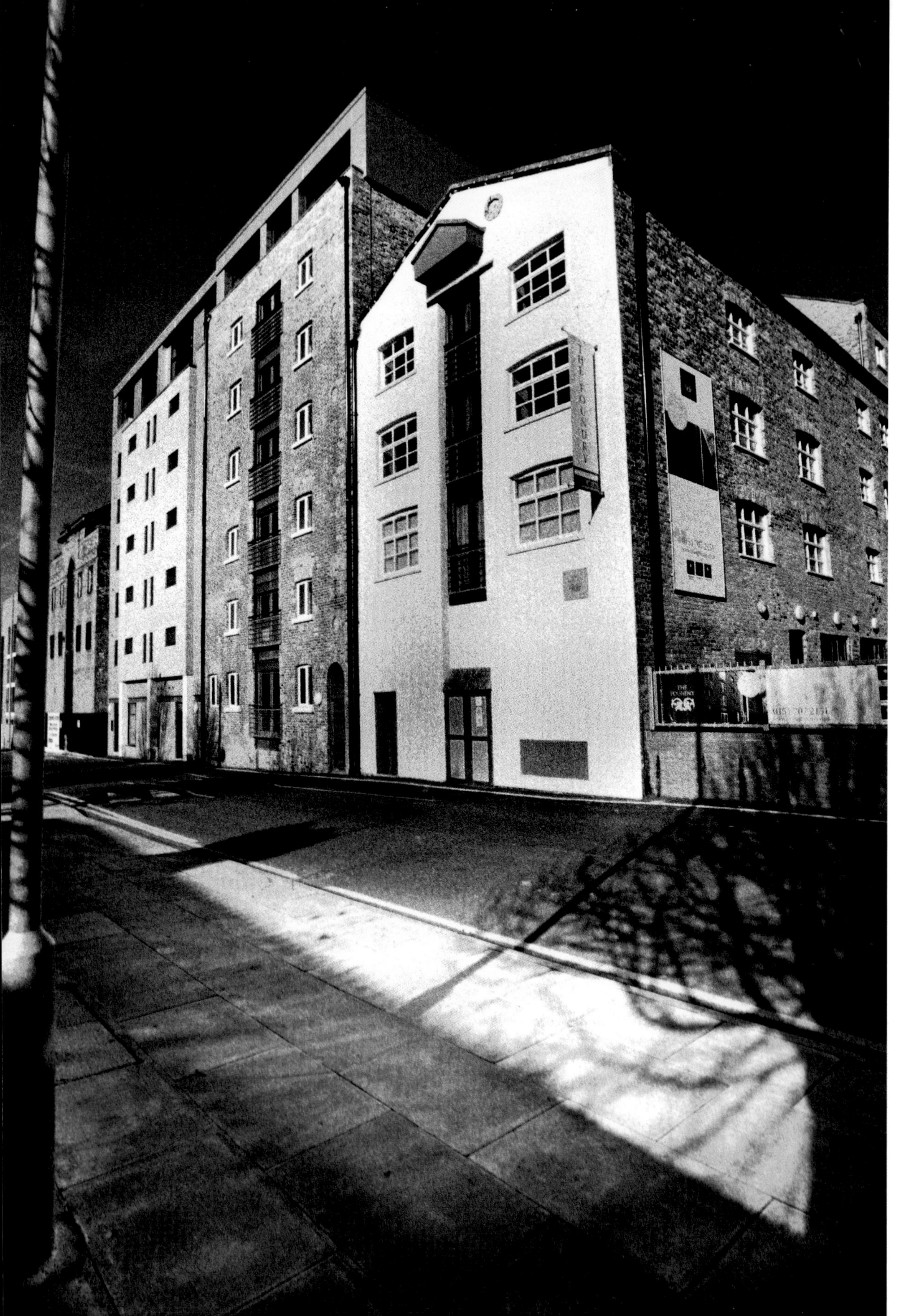

FEBRUARY 2008

'The Foundry' complex, Lydia Ann Street, completed.

APRIL 2004

Apartment/office building on Campbell Square, Brock Carmichael Architects, completed 2002

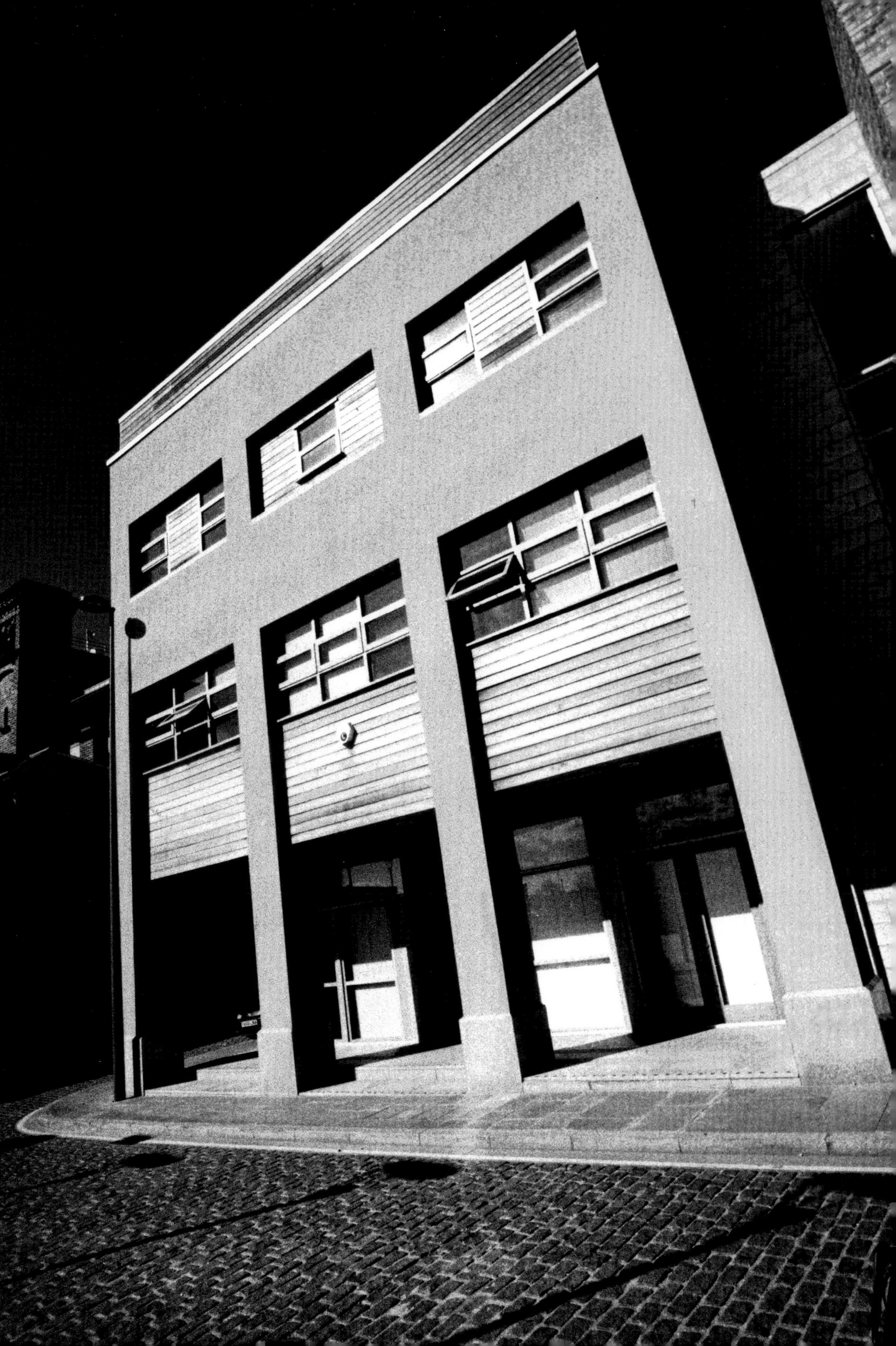

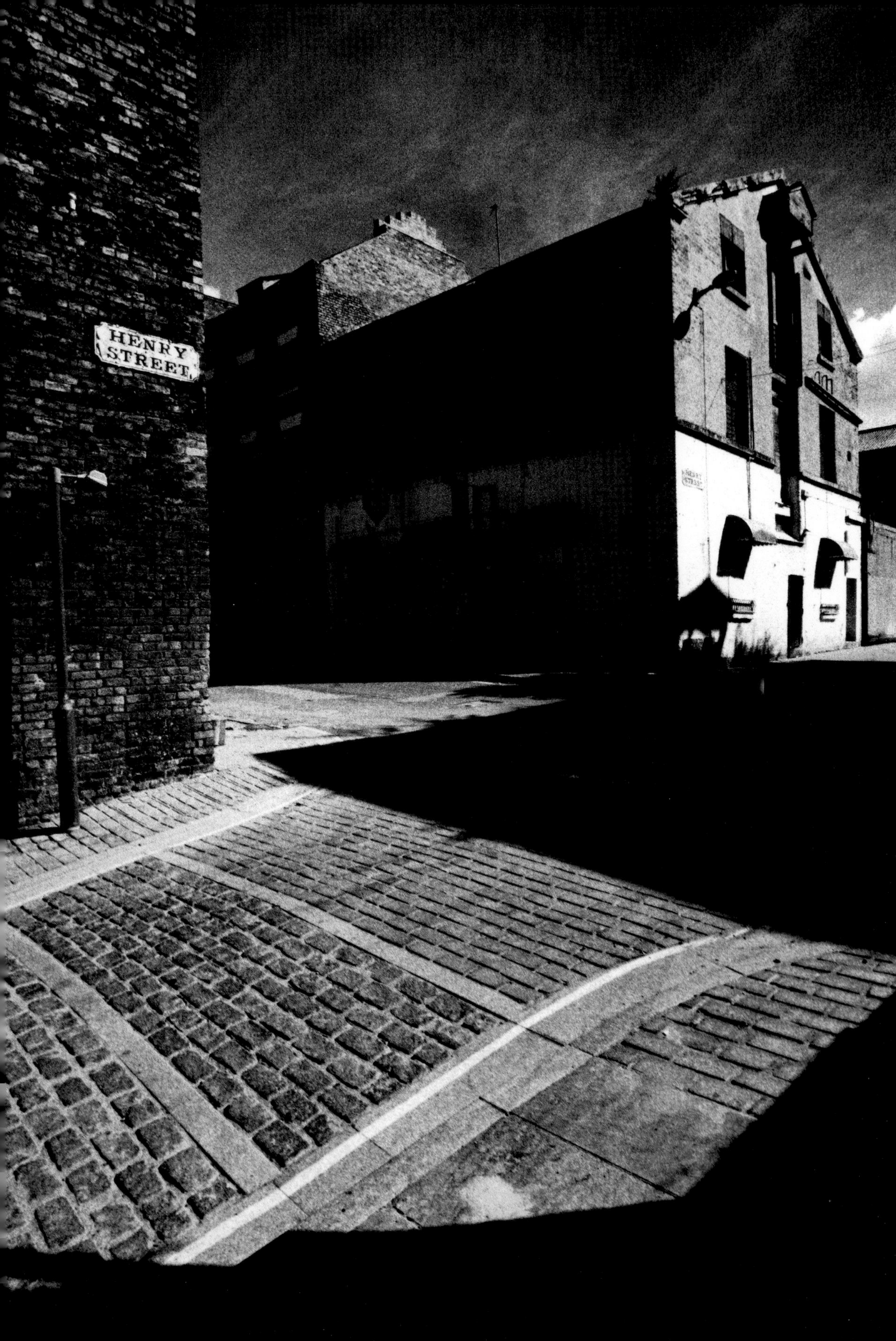

AUGUST 2001

Warehousing in Henry Street

JUNE 2000

Henry Street; still, and apparently untouched. The sunlight that gives life to the plants growing from the building's surface also washes the brick with the innumerable little shadows that animate the scene. Light and stillness are the only presence here – the warehouse is made unreal by the lack of maintenance or movement, any of those signs of human life that transform an arrangement of bricks and mortar into real architecture. Henry Street began the decade like this, waiting for the scene to change, for the movement to begin.

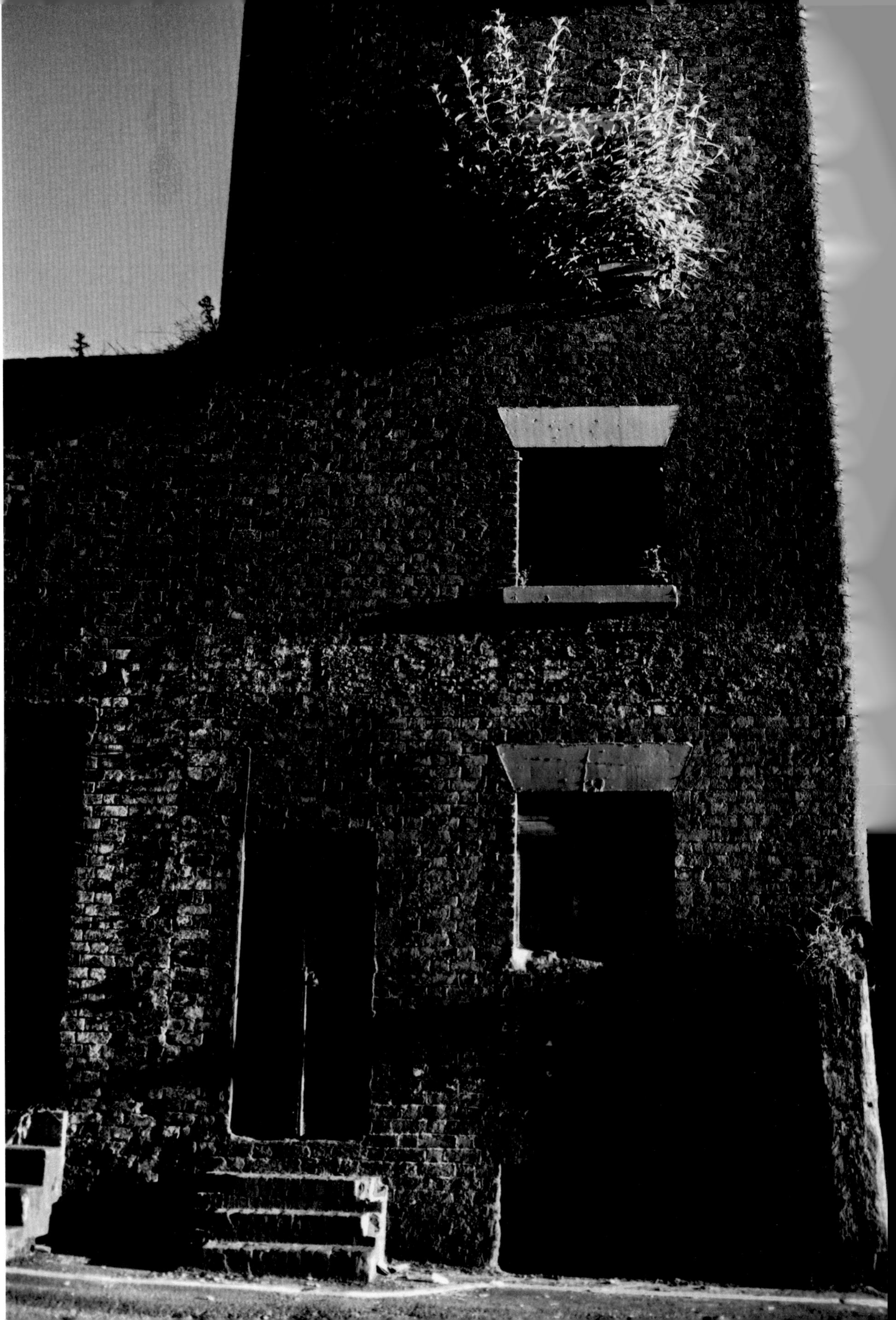

Dock Road

How do cities express their purpose through building? Every city has housing and shops, places of work, industry, leisure and all the accoutrements of urban life. Every city is a place where people gather together to live, work and share their lives. Every city has these commonalities, and their buildings reflect these shared purposes. Despite this, cities differ in substantive ways. London is, quite evidently, not the same as Moscow, nor Exeter the same as Dublin. Each city can be considered different from all others because each place has come into existence for its own reasons, operates within the boundaries of its own culture on its own terms, and is bound, therefore, to express this difference, despite the thread of similarity that binds them all together.

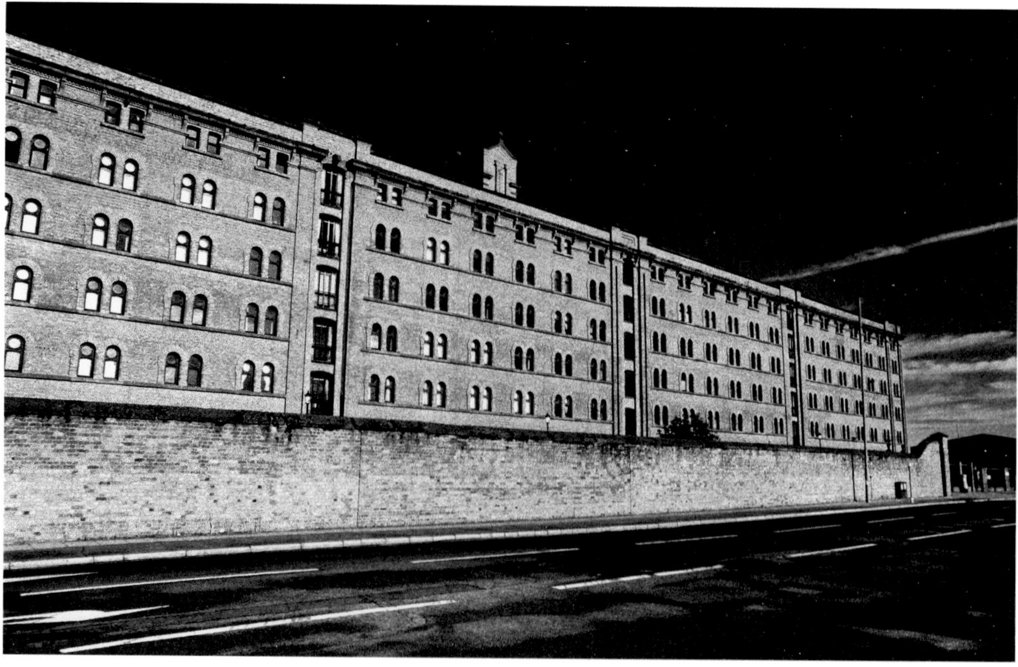

The special reason for Liverpool's growth, and why it now lies at the centre of a metropolitan region of over one million inhabitants, is the fact that it is a seaport. Regardless of its rows of housing, church spires, retail parks and office blocks which might be found in countless other places, Liverpool has the legacy and current life of its port to claim as unique to itself. Other port cities may share some of the same character – warehouses and docks are not peculiar to Liverpool – but this particular arrangement of buildings along the Mersey, with their particular history, circumstances of origin and ambition, can only ever be claimed for this city.

This is Liverpool's extraordinary place. This is the district that, more than any other in the city, creates an atmosphere of clear purpose, boldly expressed. Here are the buildings that can arrest a visitor and demand that they orientate themselves and adjust to a highly distinctive landscape. Not that there are many visitors to this part of the city, because the conventional attractions that might prompt a trip are largely absent. What there is to be seen is the unconventional beauty of muscular, functional architecture. There is dilapidation here, but also functioning silos, warehouses and quaysides. There is Victorian architecture, decorative in a no-nonsense manner that appeals to modern eyes, and twentieth-century buildings that wear their unapologetic functionalism lightly.

This extraordinary place can be seen as such in terms of its scale and form, but also as a place apart from the city. This apartness, indeed, is the essential aspect of its identity. People are absent – from the photographs, but also, in a sense, from the day-to-day life of these buildings – and this absence is indicative of the form and function of the dock road. Aside from converted commercial buildings and the scattered examples of new apartment blocks, there is no legacy of housing here, nothing, indeed, on a human scale where it is conceivable that people would have lived. Houses can be found nearby, just inland, and the people on whom these docks depended, some of them at least, lived there. The commercial significance of these docks immediately to the north of the Pier Head has declined decade by decade, and especially after the mid-1970s when containerisation and the construction of the Seaforth container port much further downstream left only a limited usefulness for these older, smaller berths. Those inland houses have survived in patches, but have mainly been redeveloped at lower densities in scheme after scheme of slum clearance between the 1920s and 1980s. It is possible to imagine that, at one point in time, given the correct confluence of a local workforce and a buoyant traffic of tonnage through the docks, these streets and buildings would have shuddered with life, with noise and movement. Undoubtedly this was the case, but this daily flow of people through the warehouses, quaysides and cafés does not mean the people were any less absent. After all, the function of all of these buildings, ultimately, was to move goods in and out of the port, efficiently and for profit. The people that animated these streets on a daily basis during the most labour-intensive period of the port's history were, after all, just hands, the fleshy components of the machine. Now that the volume of goods passing through this section of the docks has radically declined, the old machine has been stripped down, leaving only the modern equipment that still serves a purpose and older buildings that must find new uses or crumble. This is as much industrial archaeology as it is a working dockside.

Here is a landscape of unplanned grandeur, where the survivals of splendid, nineteenth-century dockland architecture mingle with gaps and replacements. All the buildings here share the same rationale of functionalism, though some have more pretension than others in how this raw purpose is dressed. The bombastic vision of Jesse Hartley of course looms large among the more impressive dockland structures, but almost by default there is an aspiration towards the monumental and the civic among all of these buildings. It is the scale of construction here that unifies everything into a single, grand composition. Everything is in situ because it has, or had, a purpose. There was never a master plan to develop the docks, let alone to create a set of buildings that would impress with their stylised solidity. Instead there were any number of individual projects, each with their own vision and reason, and each responding to a need that had arisen for more berths, more storage or any other dock-related purpose. Function is the only guiding principle here, function giving rise to impressive scale, and scale unifying these disparate buildings into a satisfying whole.

Without those houses, shops, schools and everyday buildings that give a typical character to the urban environments we are most familiar with, a place such as this will remain forever apart from the city in our minds. In many ways, the dock road is a zoo of buildings, with large, exotic forms penned together in an artificial way, set aside from the people and created for commercial gain. This separateness is its strength and value. In a very tangible sense, this extraordinary place defines what Liverpool is.

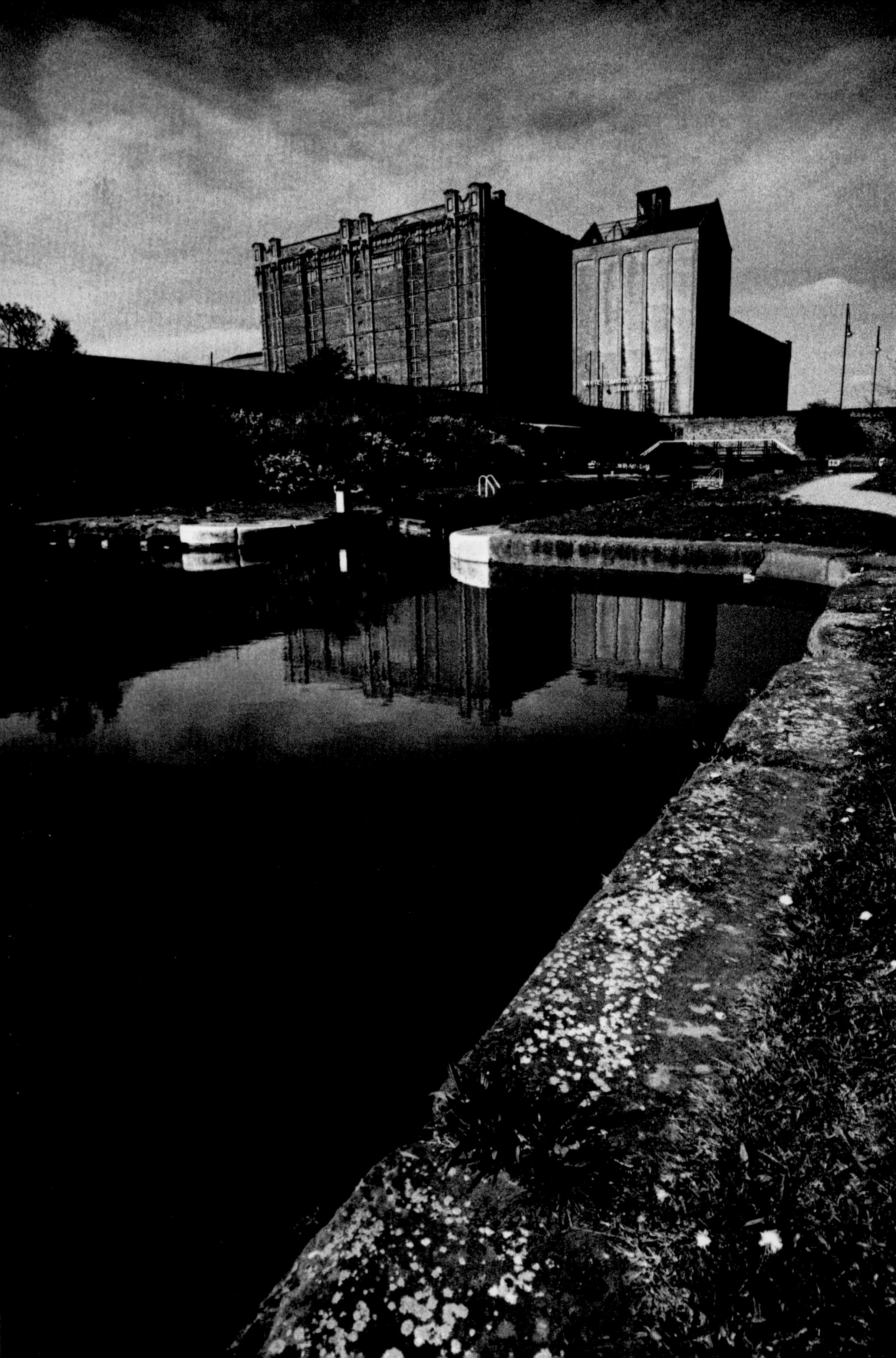

APRIL 2004

Foreground: Part of the lock system connecting the Leeds & Liverpool canal to Stanley Dock, Jesse Hartley, 1848
Background: Tobacco Warehouse, A.G. Lyster, 1897–1901

The blank-walled citadel of the tobacco warehouse stands, or stood, as a monumental entry and exit point for goods moving between the Liverpool docks and the national canal system. The picturesque dilapidation of this scene makes it seem acutely unreal; the wonder, perhaps, is in questioning how something so extraordinary was built at all, rather than asking why its decline should look like this. Accepted wisdom has it that the tobacco warehouse is the largest single brick-built structure in the world, with around 27 million bricks involved in its construction, but this is a building not dependent on the veracity of such statements. Standing with a mysterious and daunting presence from an age not long past, but still remarkable in its survival, the tobacco warehouse explains itself well enough through its name, for sight alone may not ever decipher the reason why something so improbably majestic could ever have been built.

OCTOBER 2004

Dock wall at Nelson Dock, Jesse Hartley, 1848

Nelson Dock is one of a sequence completed by Jesse Hartley in 1848 and, like the others, is defined on its inland flank by the solidity of Hartley's granite rubble walls, part of a chain of defensive barriers that stretch the length of the dock road. Initially required under the Warehousing Act of 1803 as part of the 'closed-dock' system for storing goods under bonded (duty-free) terms, insurmountable walls became the public face of Liverpool's docks throughout the course of the nineteenth century.

This is the very point where the common life of Liverpool meets the other-worldliness of the docks. This sense is underlined by the overbearing height of the wall with the clear message that what lies beyond is not for the streets to see and not for people to enter. The romance of the granite, too – the hardest stone in organic, rigid arrangement – and of the artisan-inflected name and date stone position this wall beyond the everyday. There is an unforced simplicity here that is beguiling, especially to modern eyes. Hartley was an engineer with an artist's eye, and there can be little doubt that the functional aims of his dock work were done true justice with an aesthetically elevated treatment such as this.

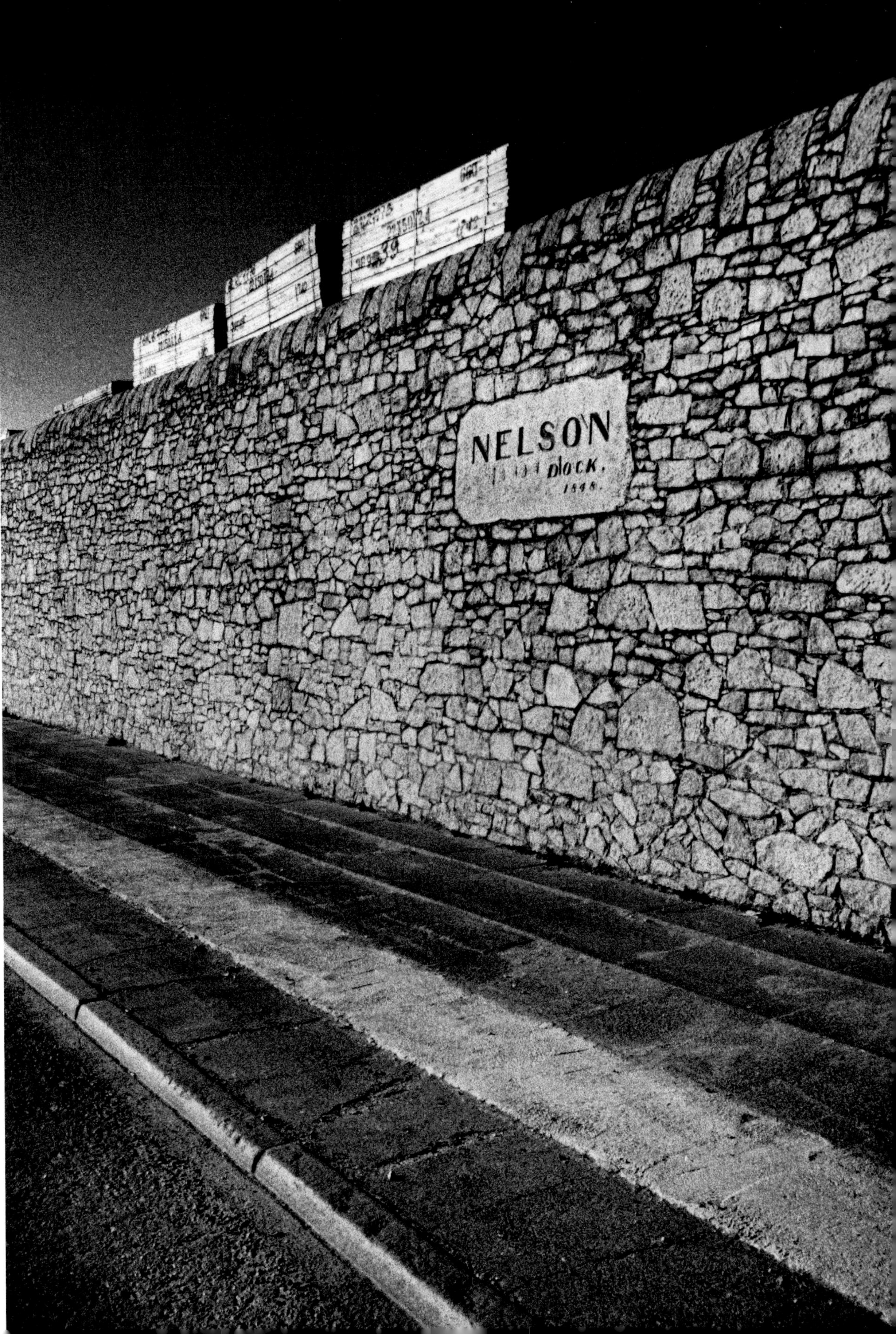

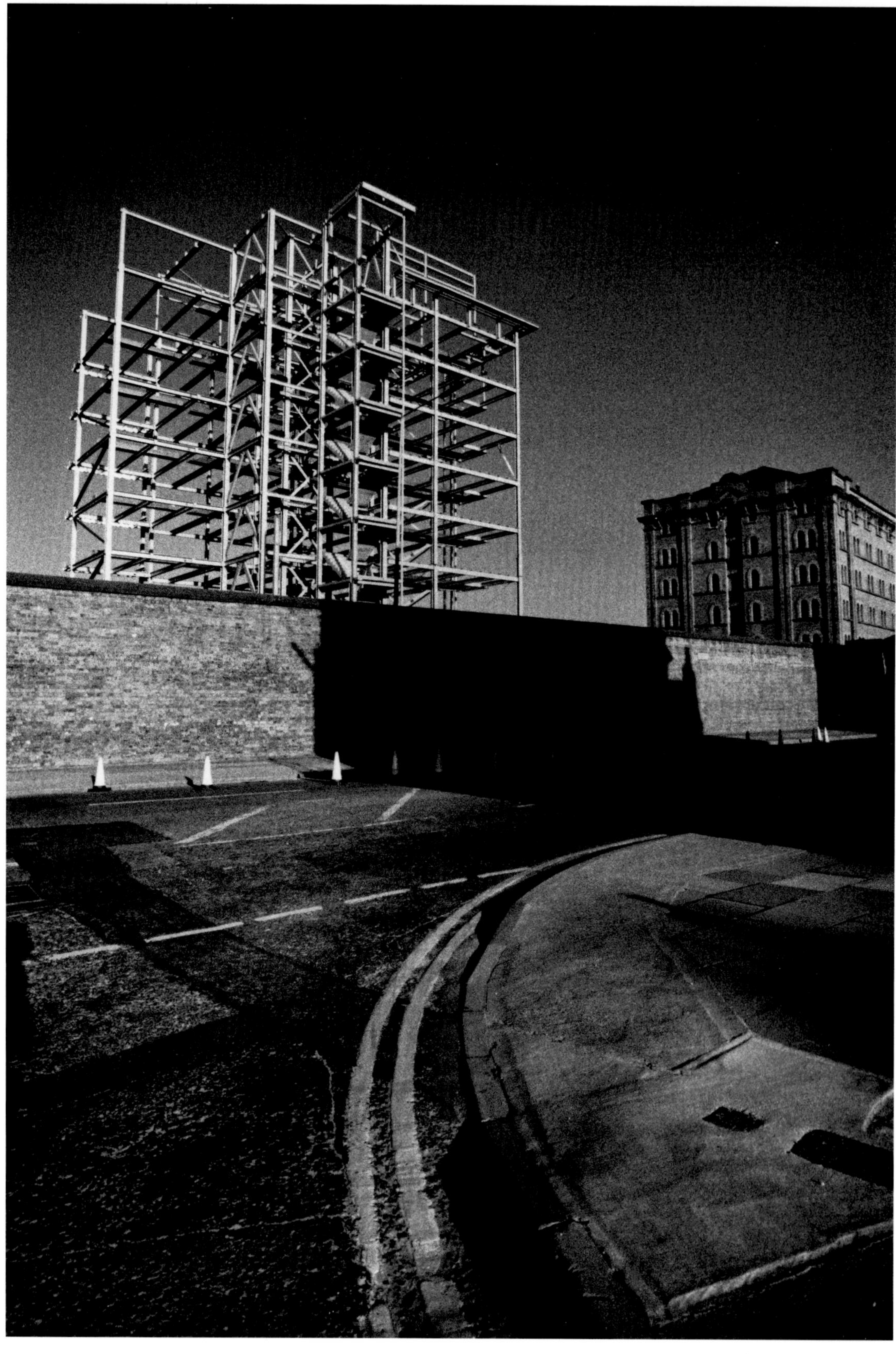

APRIL 2007

From left to right: Steel frame for 'Half Tide Dock' apartment block, Princes Half-Tide Dock, Conran and Partners, 2006–08; Waterloo Grain Warehouse, Waterloo East Dock, G.F. Lyster, 1866–68, converted into flats by Kingham Knights Associates, 1989–98

The regeneration of Liverpool's dockland from the 1980s onwards is a familiar story, but beyond the headline projects at the Albert Dock and the waterways and warehouses immediately adjacent to the city centre, there is much scope remaining for further development and reuse and the pace appears to be quickening.

Here, the rhythm of height along the dock road is picked up by a new apartment block under construction. The Romanesque windows of Lyster's grain warehouse loom up behind the dock wall, full of solemnity and redolent of an imperial, ambitious trade in commodities. The greatest commodity now dealt in by this part of the dock network is location – waterside plots, river and city views can all be packaged up and sold for profit. Broadly speaking, this is a happy switch in trading patterns. An economic boom of the past cannot simply be re-imagined, and these spaces must have new kinds of money if they are to be maintained and respected.

JUNE 2001

Tate and Lyle sugar silo, viewed from Derby Road, Tate and Lyle Engineering Department, 1955–57

A bold utilitarianism announces itself and the arrival of the post-war world at the docks in a form that subverts the cubic traditions of the past with a new shape. This parabolic swoop is so characteristic of the atomic 1950s, symbolic of the possibilities of difference that the post-war world offered. There is a fine line here between what is functionally necessary in order to store sugar, what is an excited expression of the gymnastics of reinforced concrete, and an artistic expression of boldness, newness and a wonder in what is possible. Though this building sits like a cathedral in its own dockyard close, uncrowded by near rivals, the scale matches that of buildings with a similar underlying excitement in the possibilities and needs of their own time. Recently, this building has played host to live music events; the intrinsic excitement of its architecture (let alone its cavernous interior space) is surely a superb fit for the unabashed, loud optimism of pop. The roadside wall and decorative railing is a well-meaning but wrong-headed exercise in heritage-making, part of a 1990s landscaping effort to attract new businesses to the area. Stolid and unremarkable this work may be, but when contrasted directly with the sugar silo, it looks markedly inappropriate.

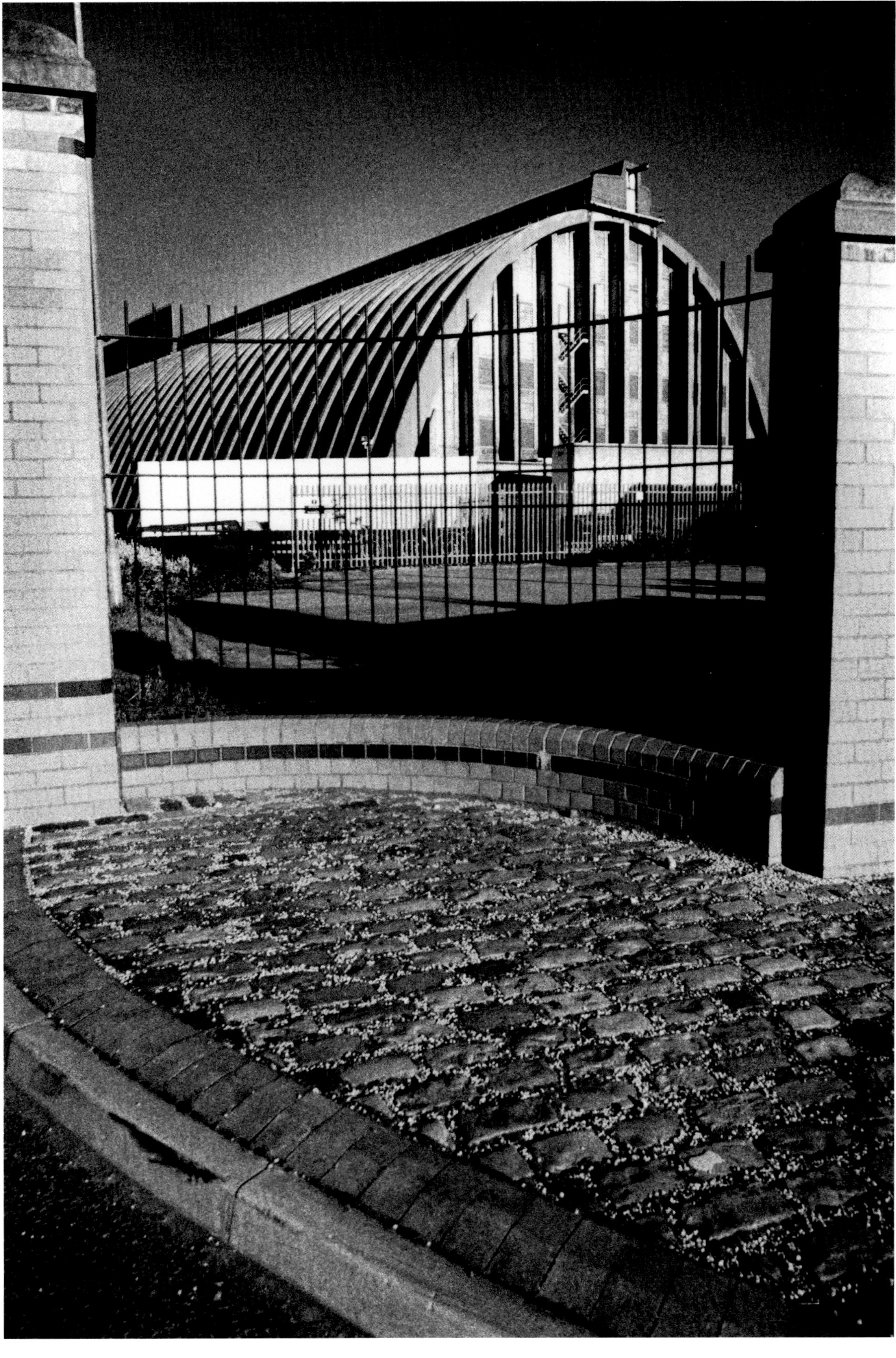

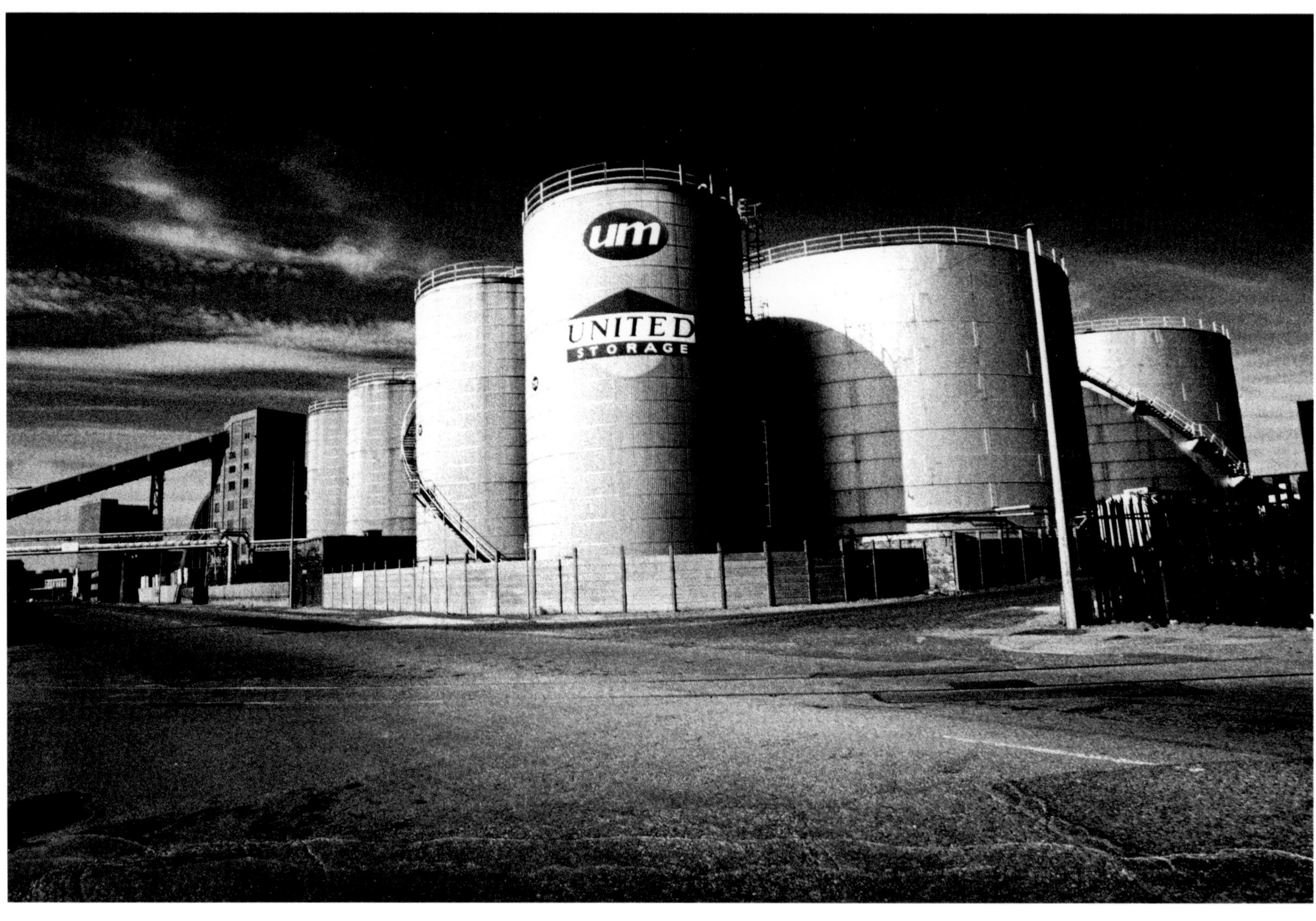

JUNE 2001

Silos for United Storage, once
part of the Tate and Lyle complex.

JULY 2006

From left to right: City Lofts apartment block, Conran and Partners, 2005–07; multi-storey car park, KKA Architects, completed 2005

At Princes Dock, the dock road runs into the city centre and dockland becomes part of Liverpool's commercial district. In common with many of the nineteenth-century docks built in the city, Princes never had substantial buildings along its quayside, hosting only transit sheds and a railway station for the transatlantic passenger trade that was not to survive the process of change. Located so conveniently close to the city centre, Princes is gradually becoming a watery version of the same, with car parks, apartments, hotels and offices jostling for a position on the quayside, the land there for the taking.

Here, a prosaic but badly needed multi-storey car park straddles the space between the water and the dock wall, beyond which lies Old Hall Street and the historic business quarter. Its height and utilitarian architecture may be fairly compared with the same principles at work in the dockside warehouses, and, despite its unprepossessing appearance, it is certainly symbolic of the new life of the docks.

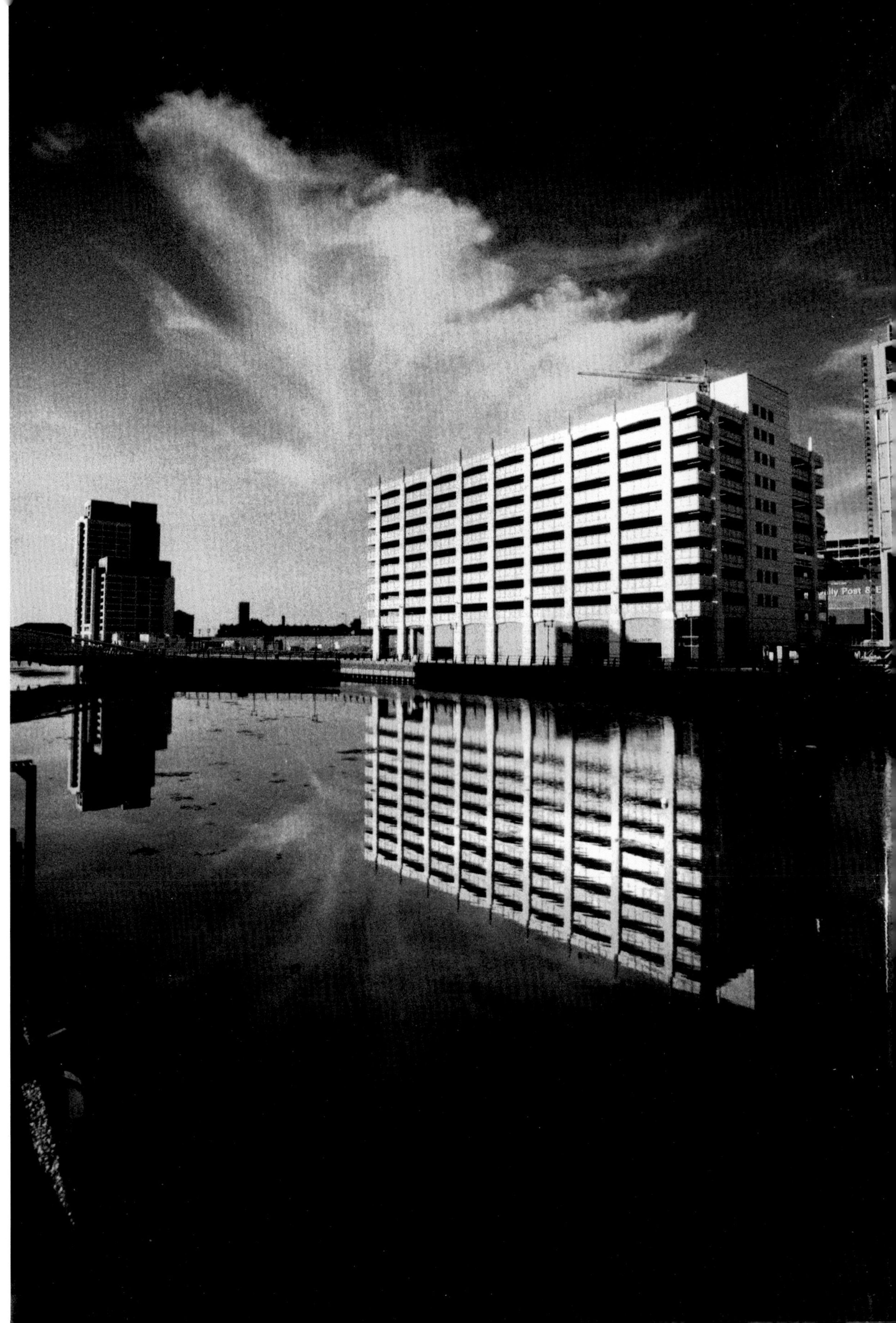

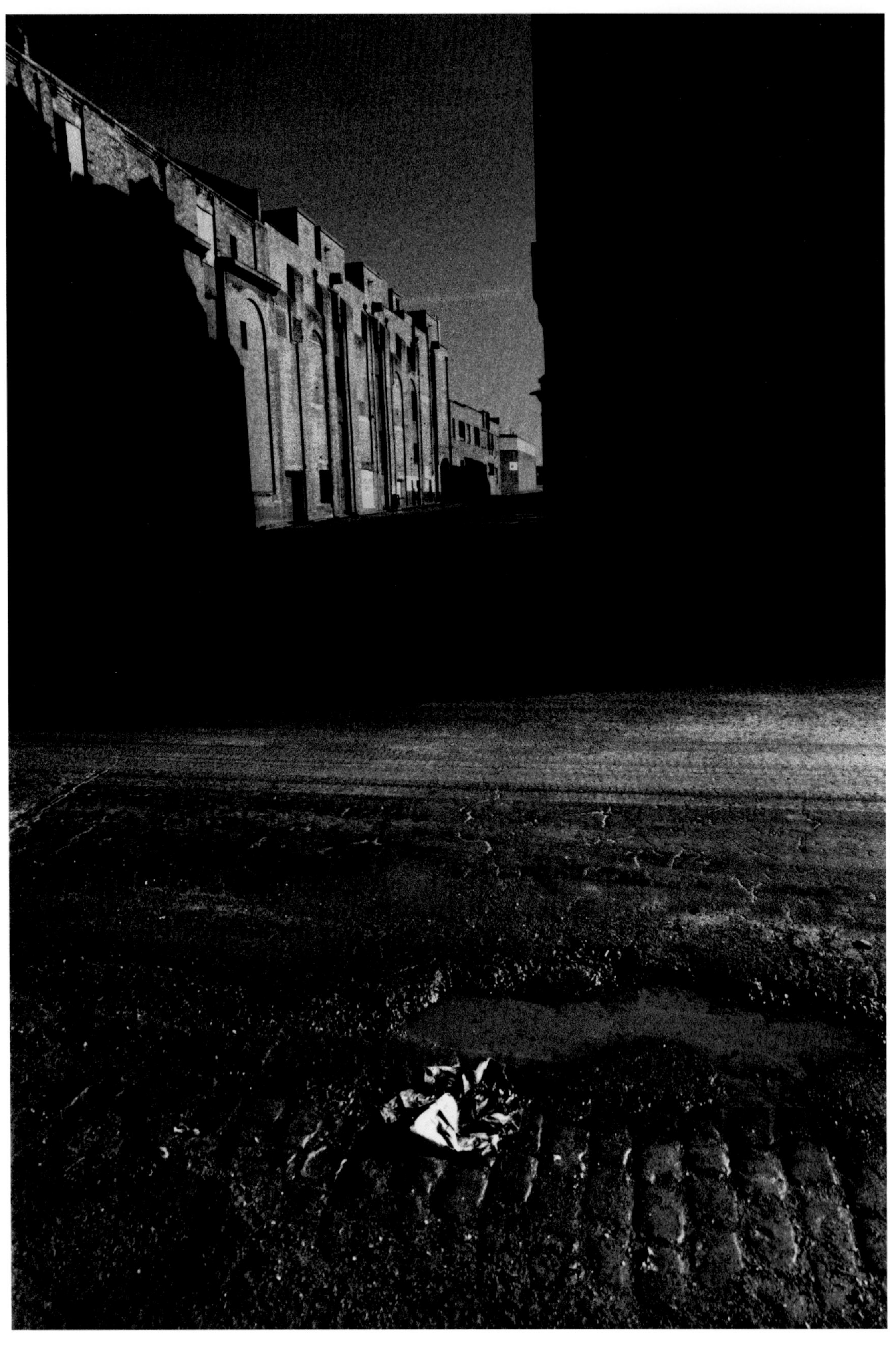

FEBRUARY 2004

Warehouses on Brunswick Street, as viewed from Regent Road

FEBRUARY 2004

Mid-nineteenth-century warehouse on Waterloo Road

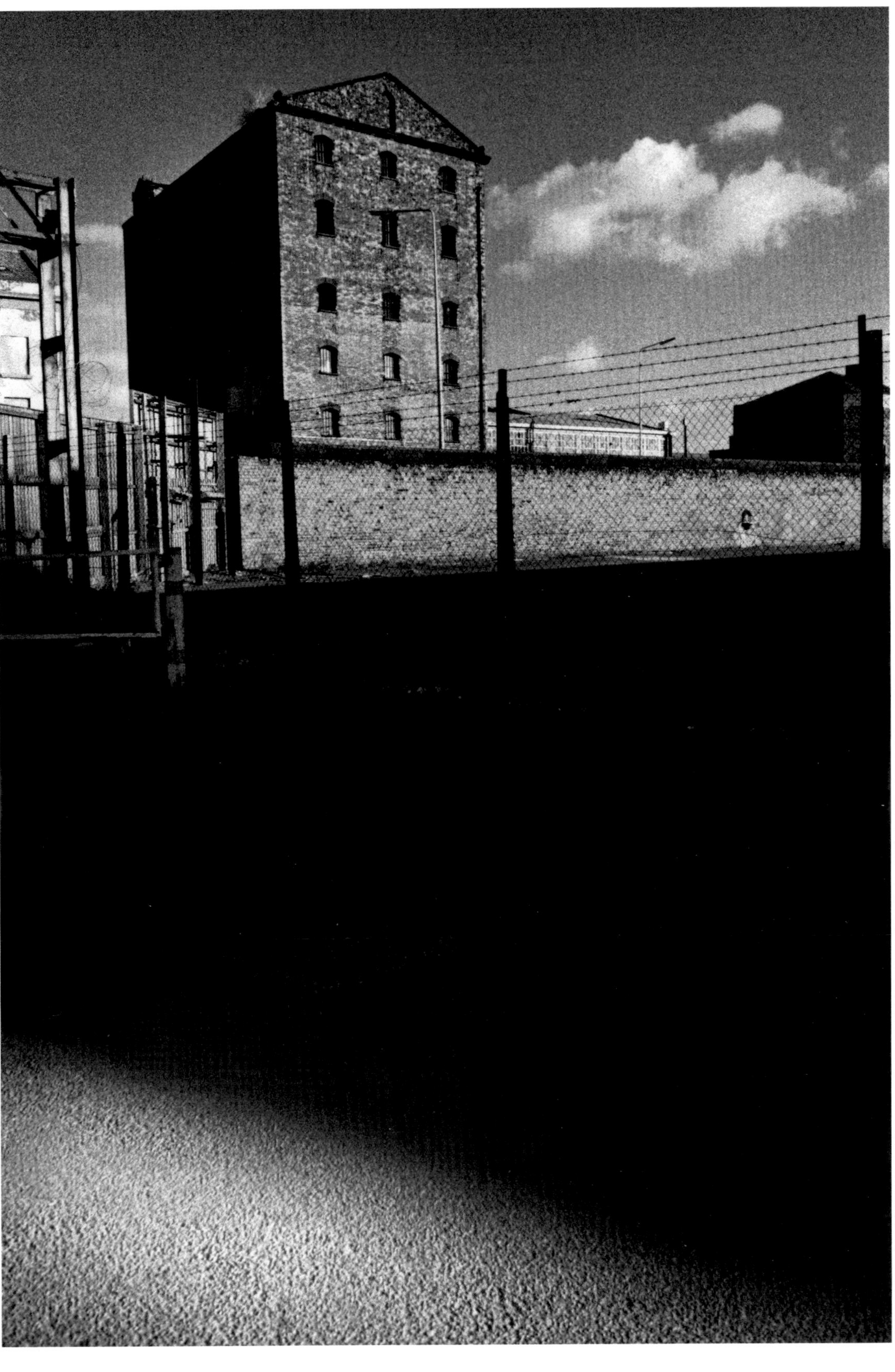

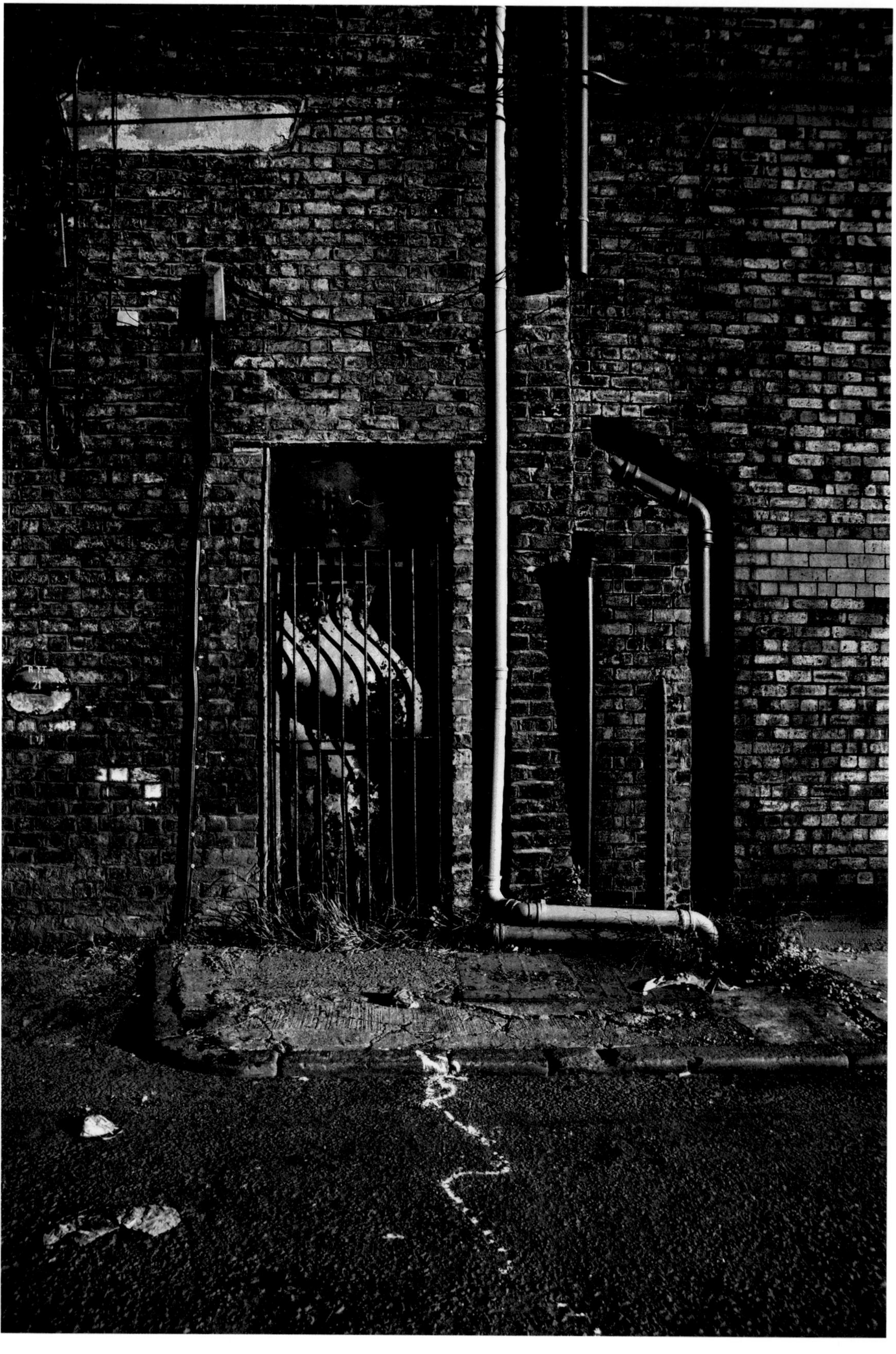

JUNE 2001

The utilitarian aspects of a modern dockland building: overlooked and neglected, but an important part of the forms and textures that give these streets their special character.

JULY 2006

From left to right: Tobacco Warehouse, A.G. Lyster, 1897–1901; Stanley Dock warehouse and boundary wall, Jesse Hartley, 1848

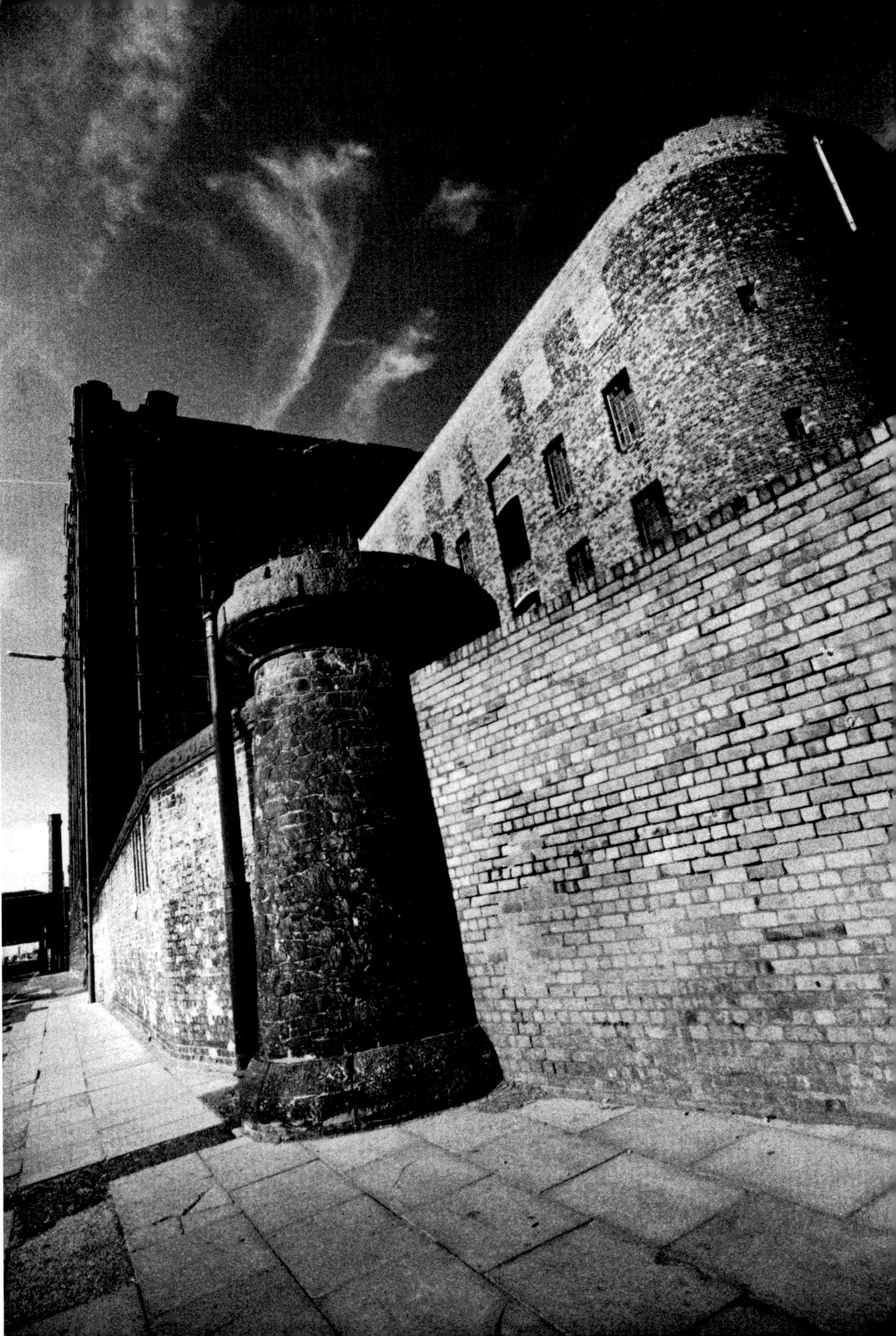

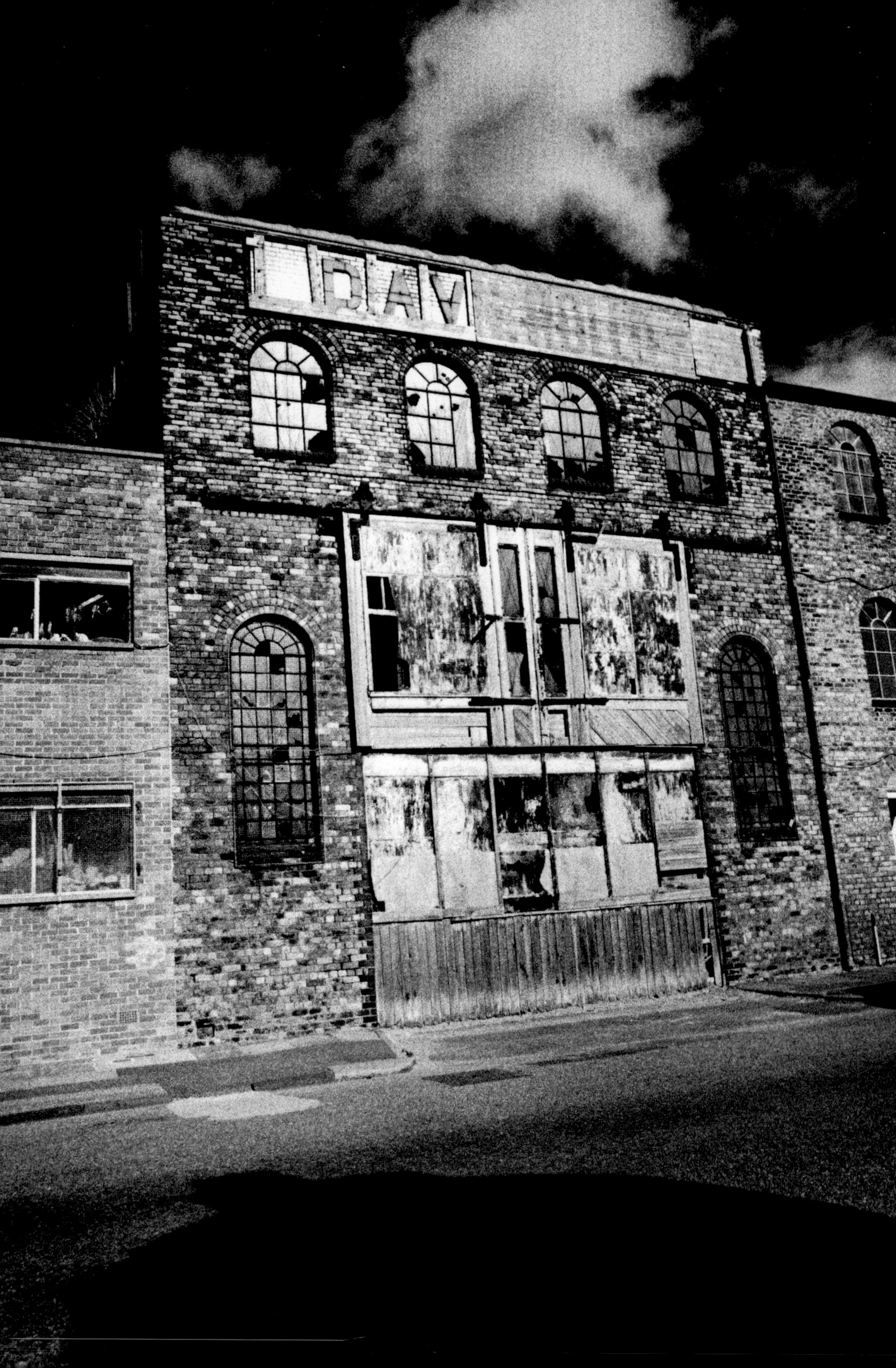

JULY 2004

Warehouse on Regent Road

MAY 2004

The functional buildings along Regent Road form, in parts, a continuous edifice, sometimes faceless, sometimes vibrant, expressing the evolving architectural styles of dockland through the decades.

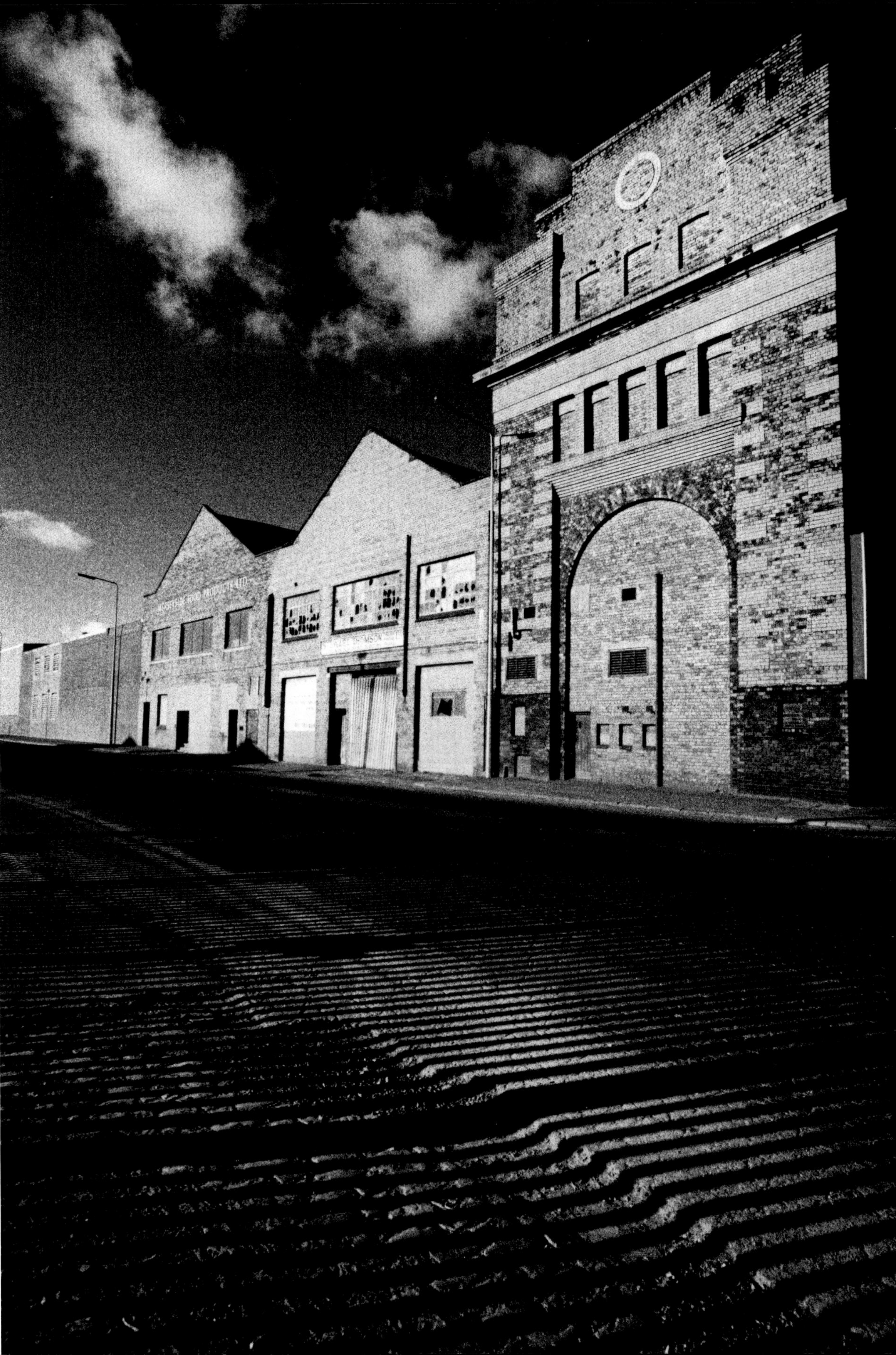

Baltic

This is a place where the culture of Liverpool resides, beside the docks and away from the offices, banks and department stores just along the road. The city centre development company, Liverpool Vision, would have potential developers call this place the Baltic Triangle, a name derived from the obvious geometry of the plan and the Baltic Fleet pub, which anchors the point where the district touches the fringes of the city centre and waterfront. It was not called the Baltic Triangle in the past, and may never be called that in the future, for this is a place slightly out of reach of names and definitions. Fundamentally, this was, and is again, a place to live. Which is to say, living in the roundest possible sense of the word. Churches, pubs, a myriad of employment opportunities in the docks and dock-related manufacturing, local shops and businesses and, above all, homes, defined this cityscape – a dense spread of buildings dedicated to living life and priming a vital economy. This was not a suburb and it was not the city centre. It was, instead, where Liverpool itself was located. Dense living, densely woven with a criss-crossing of cultures, formed a pattern of life in this district that was distinctive and that made an impact, holding an idea of Liverpool within its bounds and helping to define this idea where it existed in other parts of the city.

Baltic is the fleet, and the pub, and of course the sea, for this is a place where innumerable waters met and mingled. The Baltic meets the Arctic meets the Caribbean, and Scandinavia meets Jamaica in these streets. A rushing together of currents, warm and cold, created at once turbulence and a place of shelter. Some of the people carried by the water stayed and some flowed on, but everywhere are the traces of their passage, the cityscape carved, smoothed, raised and depressed by the diluvial effects. After this torrent, there is decimation all around – as elsewhere in the city, bombs and the decline of the traditional port make their severe effects felt – but a spirit of place remains here in the streets, the bricks and the sky. This was a place of exoticism and danger, of poverty and opportunity, of local sentiment and global reach. These things do not disappear completely; the streets, the bricks and the sky recall their meaning. In some instances, they do not disappear at all.

This is an heroic piece of the city, still. In parts gigantic, the buildings reach up and fill the air, matching – reinforcing – the scale of the sky and the river. In parts, size is subsumed by mystery and a disconcerting sense of other places and times. In their edited form, largely bereft of people and noisy activity, the landmarks carry a heavy weight of conveying identity, and mix uneasily together. This can be a curious place with both buildings and empty spaces feeling as though they don't belong. Terraces of houses and shops along and around the spine of Park Lane and St James Street have long been eradicated, while the stately avenues of warehousing along Jamaica Street are now thinned by changing needs into a broken chain. Warehouses that once helped to maintain a tall, undulating skyline of gables and winches now stand as brave survivals, their blank brick walls stretching up and out like the remaining pages of an antiquarian book, fanned out and discarded.

In places, the gaps are filled with signs of replacement and the sense of a new beginning. Tall warehouses are matched with tall blocks of residential flats, a balm to soothe the loss of height and of population. Sometimes, conversions of existing buildings stake a claim on the future of this district. Whatever happens here, however, the future cannot revive the past; the social and economic metamorphosis of the years has been too profound. What is achieved instead is a convincing echo, with ideas and circumstances sufficiently similar that spectacle and opportunity are still possible here. The physical remains of the past are unsettling in their oddity and disjointedness – unsettling enough to excite and inspire – and it is among the remains, in the empty buildings, broad streets and open spaces, that the stimulus is found for regeneration. This is indeed Liverpool's frontier land, for who can ignore the opportunity afforded by cheap, neglected space so close to the reviving city centre? Once, this place was Liverpool, then it became nowhere at all, and now, at the frontier of the central area, at the conceptual frontier of everything the city believes it may become, it is a place in which Liverpool can recast itself.

The culture of the streets – of the dockers' drink and the languages and the prayer and the shouts and the stews – is become folklore. Perhaps folklore is not death, but it is not the vital culture of the future. The culture of today looks for inspiration in that folklore but also in the space in which it was played out, among the buildings that remain here. Here, culture is prompted to exist by the A Foundation, the Liverpool Biennial, the Flying Picket and others so that in cheap, ungentrified circumstances, at least art has a chance to have its say. There are performances, interventions, installations and a sense that the streets and buildings of this place must be interrogated with new eyes and new minds if they are to live again. The life, the culture, will come from this art, because it has been thought about, worked through and is a physical presence here. An investment in thought will make this district live again. Yes, the rents are cheap, and the buildings undesirably dilapidated or mundane while remaining close to the natural buoyancy of town, and this is all to the good. But more than convenience, there is responsiveness to the site and, above all, a feeling that art and music are at home here. The culture of the past is not forgotten in the art spaces and apartments that first find a foothold and then will come to define this place. How could it be forgotten when to live at the heart of Liverpool, on the edge of Western Europe, among the colours, songs and beliefs of what must have seemed like the whole world, was indeed the culture? These memories, and the attempt to reflect them back into the world with new buildings as tall as the old warehouses and art that seeks understanding in a complex and interconnected world, is enough to revive at least a sense of the past.

NOVEMBER 2006

From left to right: Light industrial buildings, New Bird Street; installation for the Liverpool Biennial of Contemporary Art, 'Hua Biao from China' (Shen Shaomin, 2006)
Background: Tower of Liverpool Cathedral, Giles Gilbert Scott, 1904–78

Thrilling juxtaposition is characteristic here, and no more so than when an art festival rolls into town. Shen Shaomin's work for the 2006 Liverpool Biennial resembles the ruins of a Chinese Palace in the most innocuous backstreet of modern, light industrial activity. Not so very away from here, Chinese sailors began to settle in Liverpool from the 1860s onwards, establishing one of the oldest Chinese communities in Europe. This Hua Biao (or totem) richly carved in marble, is hardly reminiscent of the hard-working, commonplace activities of the Liverpudlian Chinese, but in its state of collapse it tells a story beyond China and beyond Liverpool. Cultures can produce astounding achievements and can cross the seas to spread their ideas, but when time moves on, the culture of the past (and its material treasure) can be broken, misunderstood and neglected. This piece may only be representational and temporary, but it is a tangible expression of the forgotten past all around this district. The physical reminders that remain are awe- inspiring but often, out of their time, also deeply confusing.

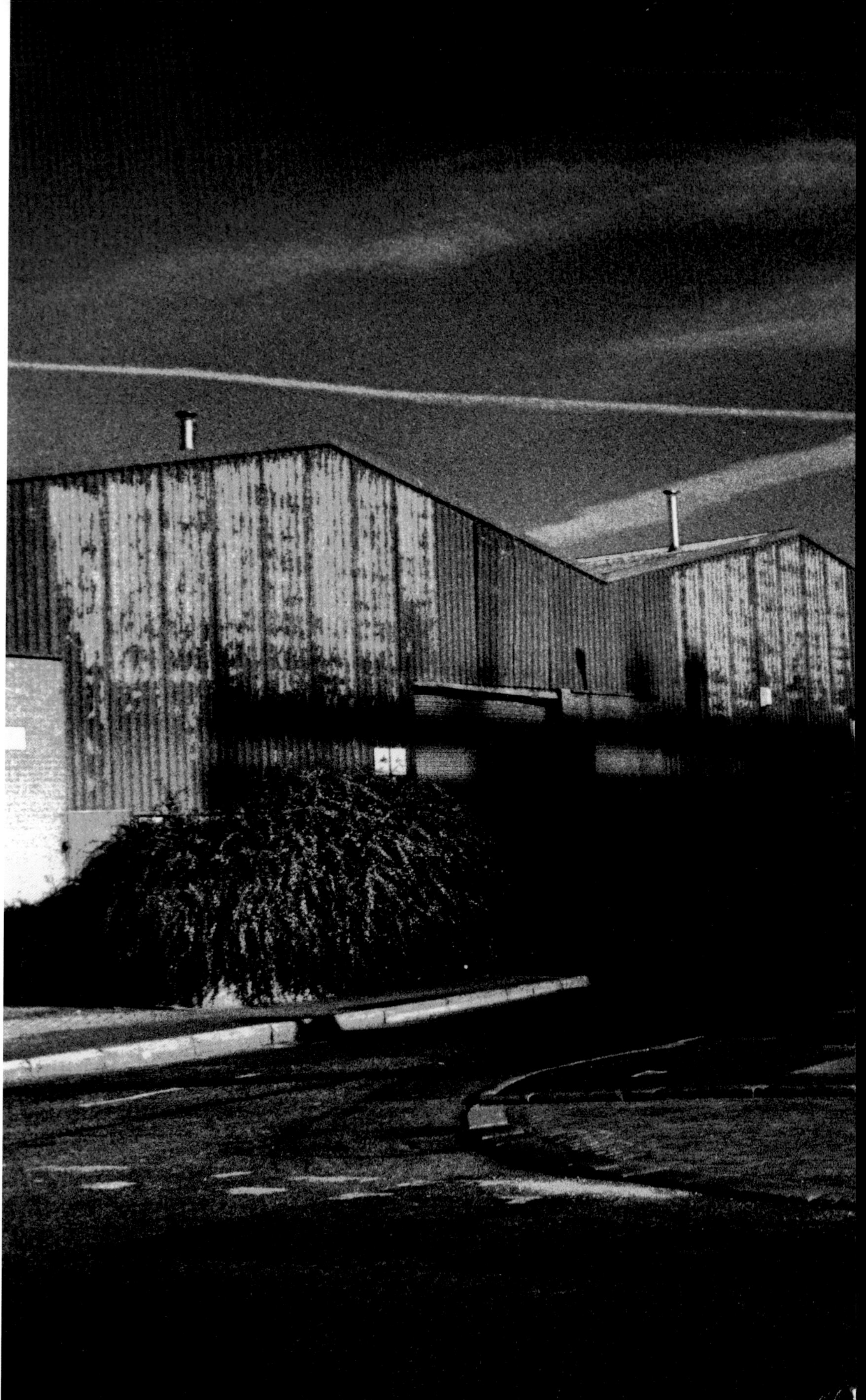

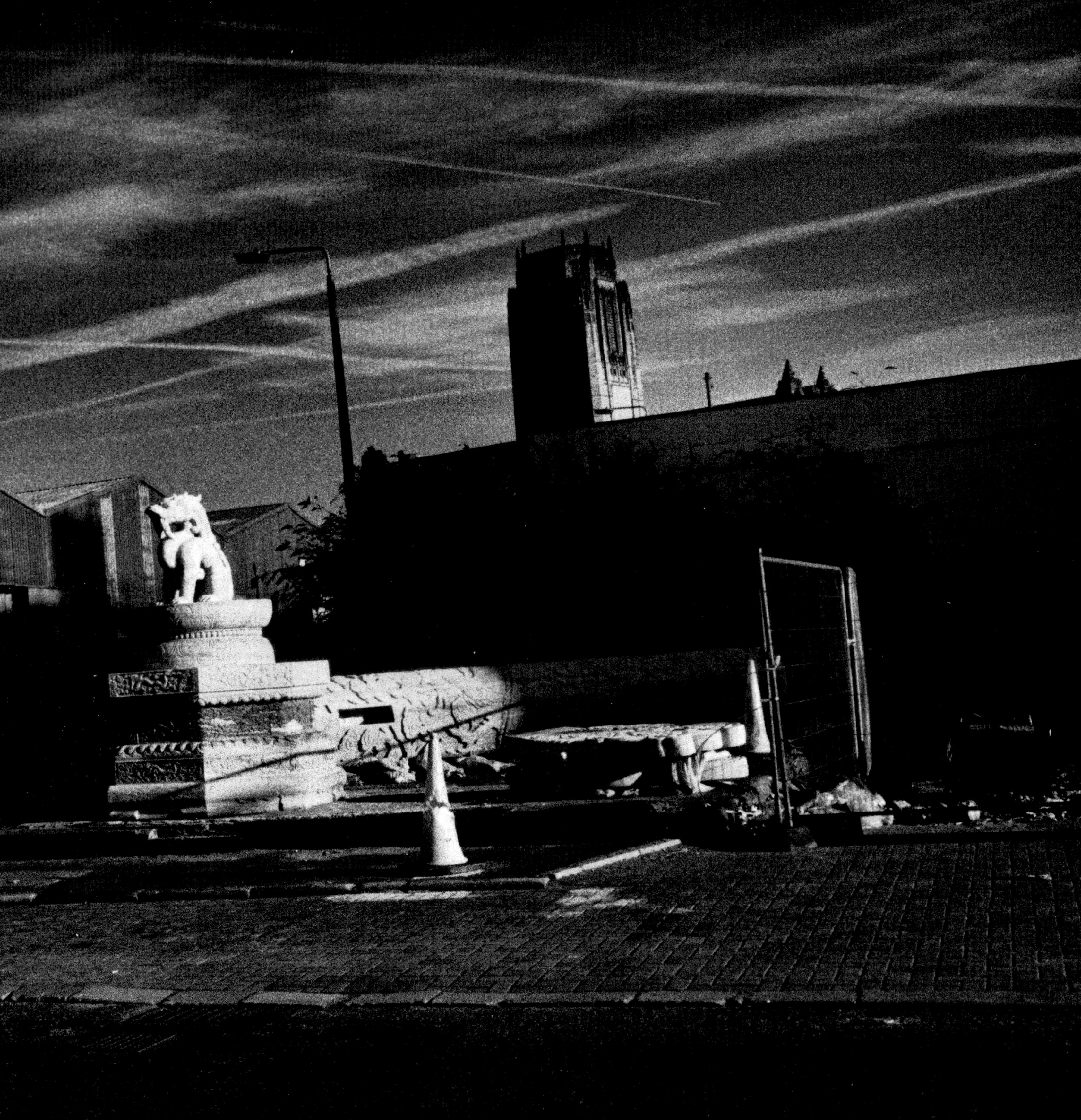

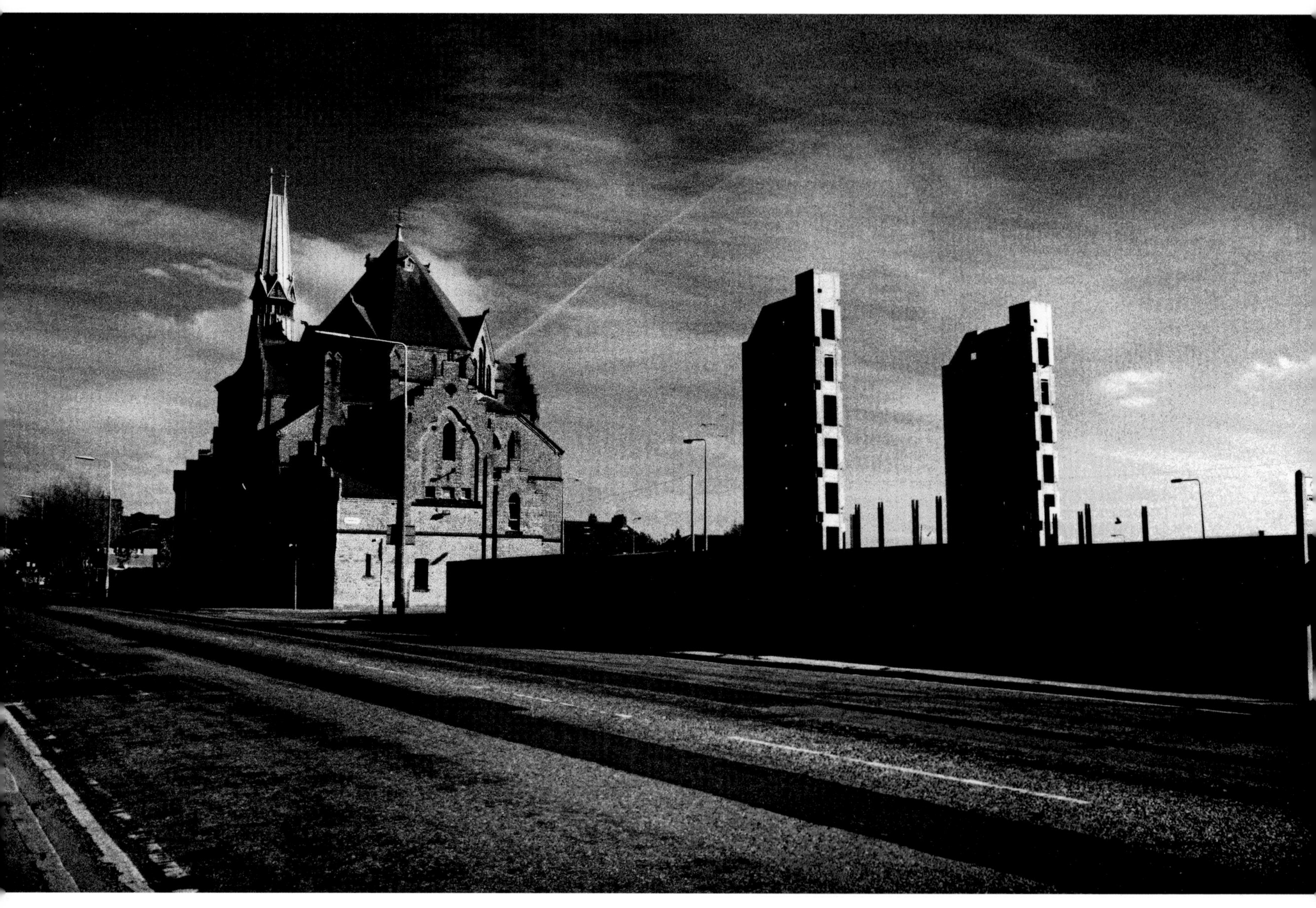

APRIL 2005

Gustav Adolfs Kyrka or Swedish Seamen's Church, W.D. Carö, 1883–84, Park Lane; lift towers in place for an apartment block in Cornhill

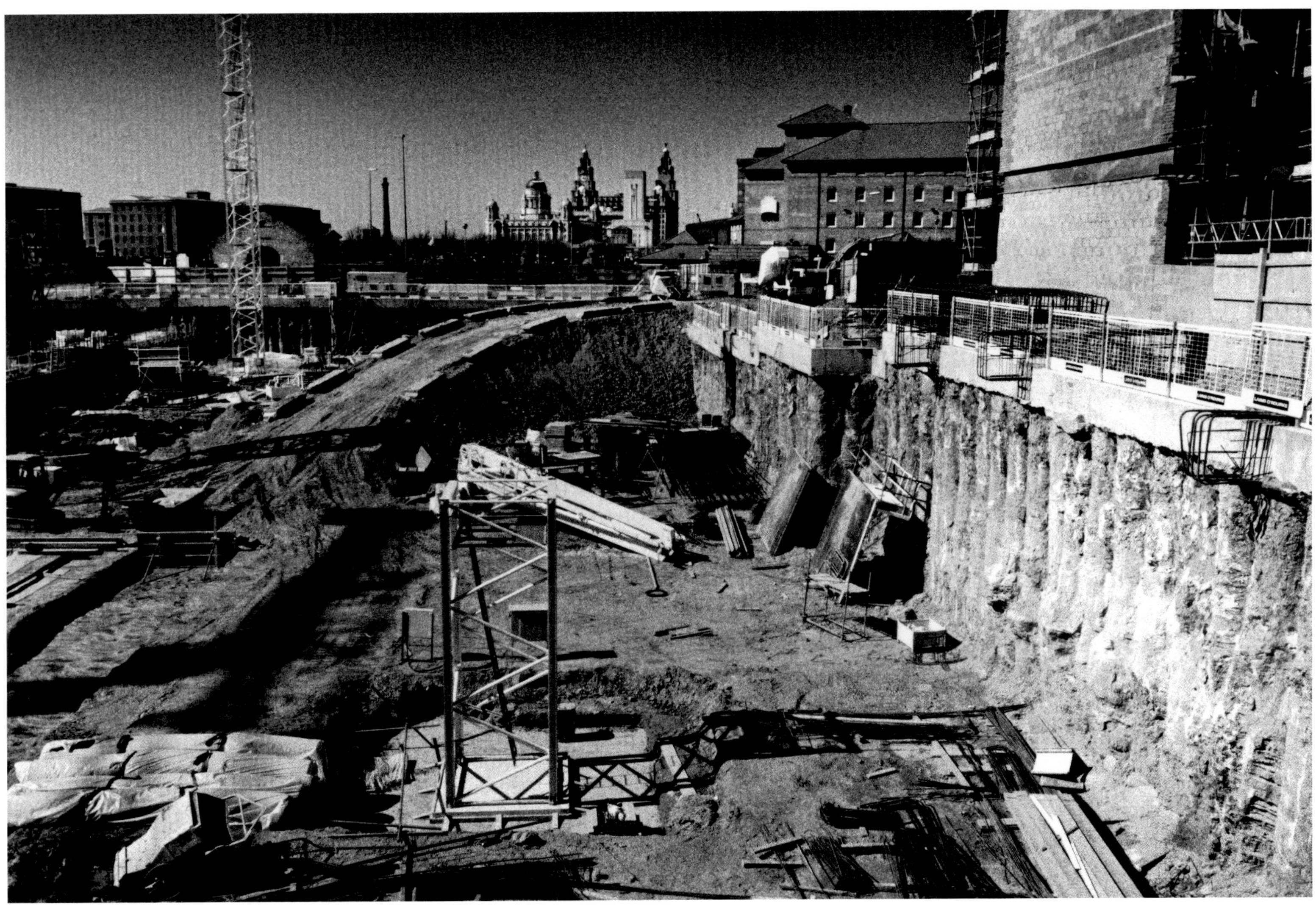

APRIL 2006

Foreground: Excavations for a hotel and leisure complex on Wapping
Background, from left to right: Albert Dock, Jesse Hartley, 1843–47; Port of Liverpool Building, Briggs and Wolstenhome/Hobbs and Thornley, 1903–07; Royal Liver Building, Walter Aubrey Thomas, 1908–11; George's Dock Ventilation Tower and Control Station, Herbert J. Rowse, 1932–34; Hotel Ibis/ Formule 1

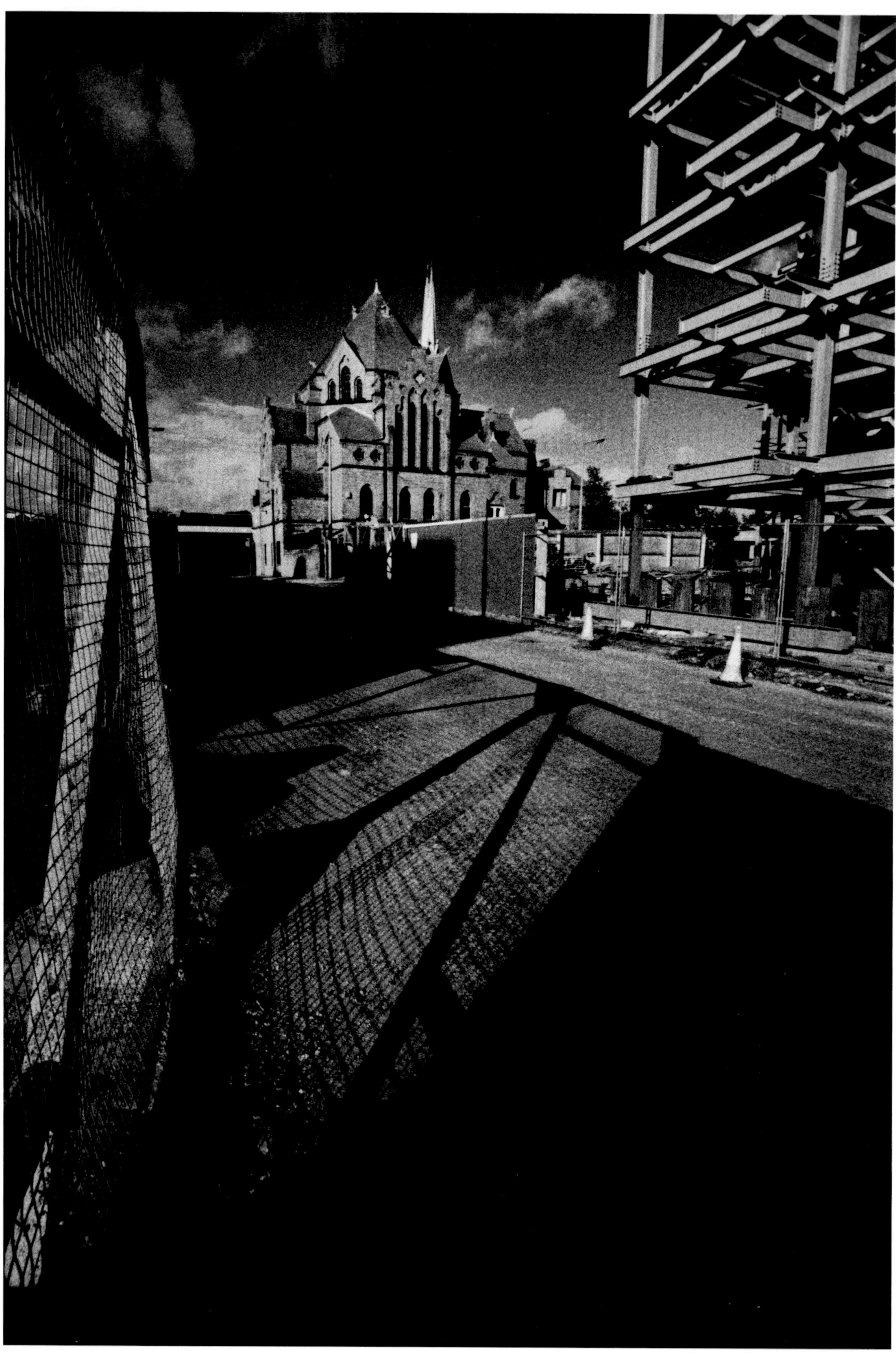

JUNE 2005

Gustav Adolfs Kyrka or Swedish Seamen's Church, W.D. Carö, 1883–84

A cheap wire and timber fence is indicative of the mundane surroundings of this arresting architectural confection. Foreign in the most obvious and wonderful way, the church is all the more noticeable for its isolation under the sky here. The steel-framed construction of new apartments has begun the process of restoring height, scale and people to this area. Perhaps Carö's work will once again enjoy the company of a busy, purposeful district.

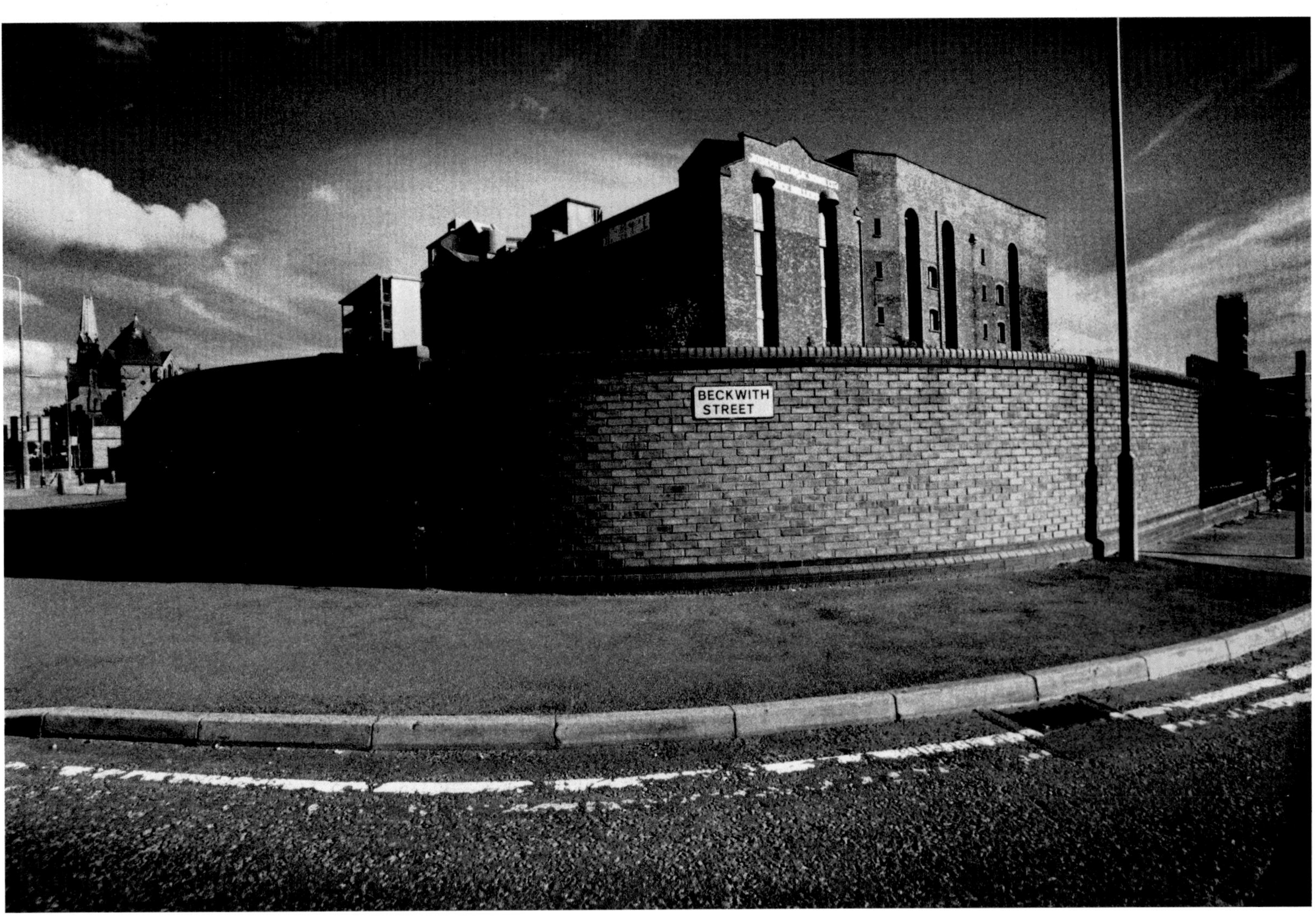

JUNE 2007

From left to right: Gustav Adolfs Kyrka or Swedish Seamen's Church, W.D. Carö, 1883–84; Heap's Rice Mill, earliest parts nineteenth century; lift tower of hotel and leisure complex on Wapping.

A boundary wall from the 1980s sets an out-of-place suburban mood on Beckwith Street. Numerous schemes to revive the area between Wapping and Chinatown have seen a range of solutions employed, all of which have failed by degrees.

Architectural fragments of these past ideas are scattered around, adding a confusing layer of fabric on top of what has been lost and beside the dislocated monuments that survive.

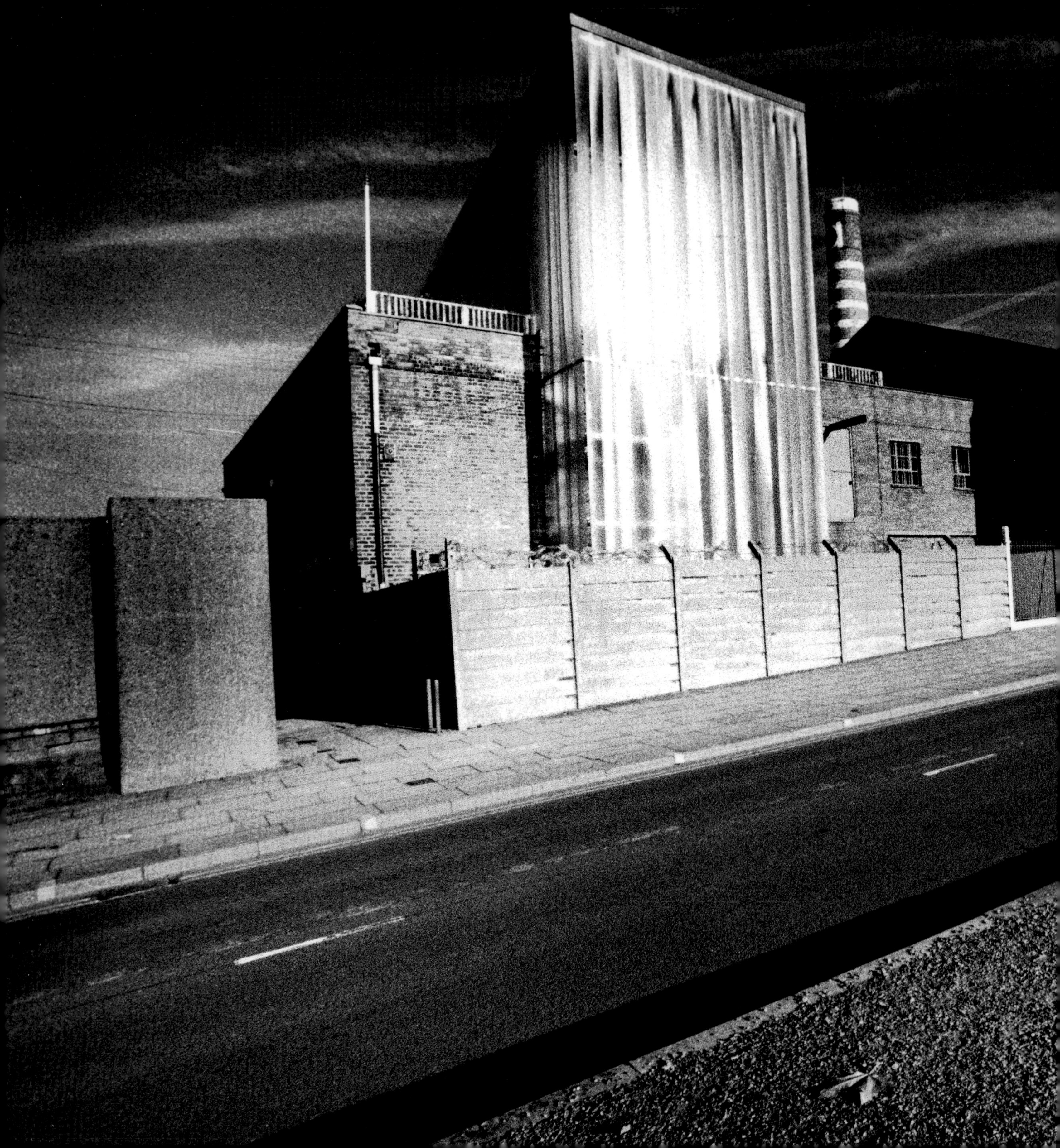

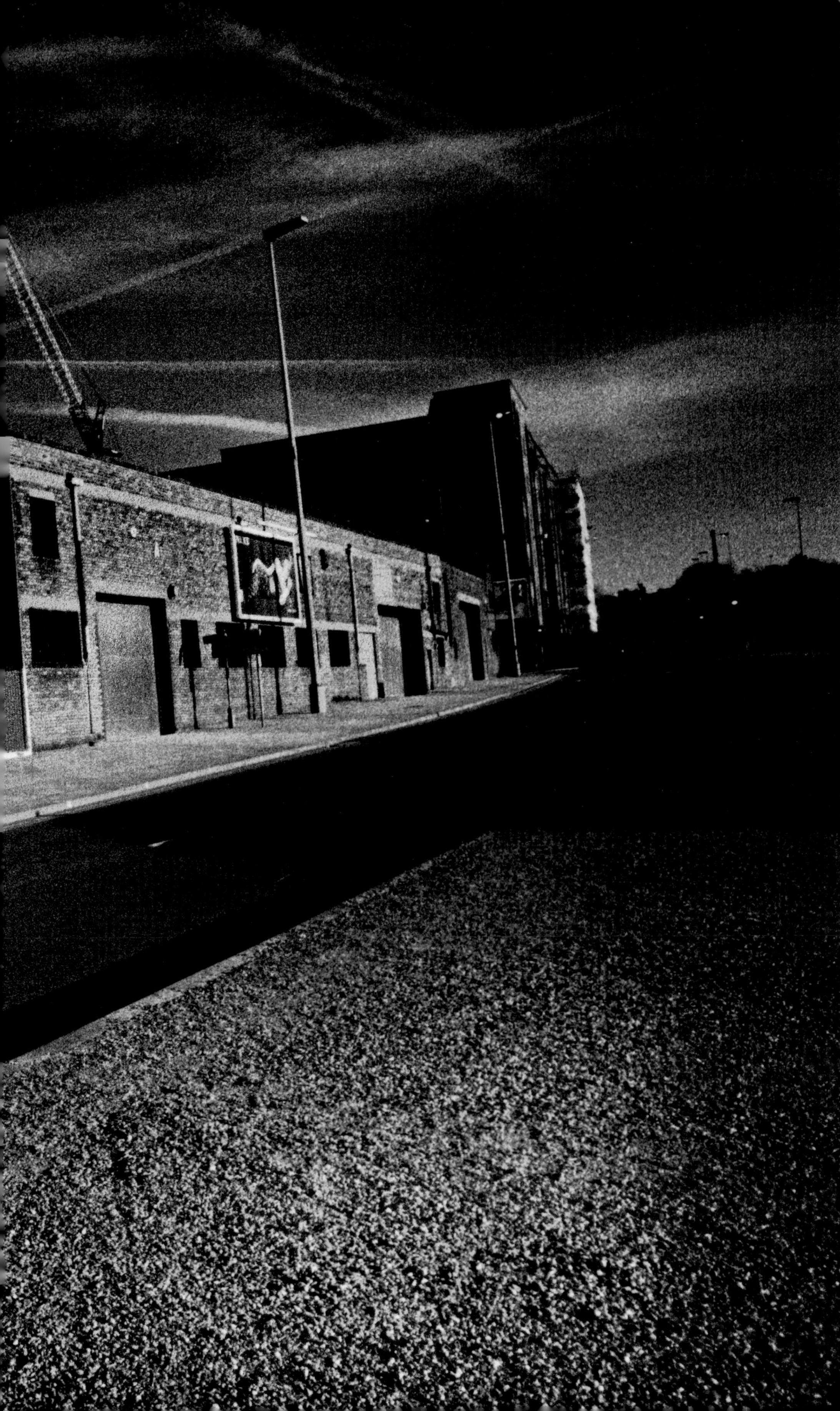

NOVEMBER 2006

The A Foundation's Greenland Street site, seen from Parliament Street. On the left is the 'Blade Factory', seen with temporary architectural intervention by Karsten Huneck and Bernd Truempler of the Office for Subversive Architecture. In the centre is 'The Furnace', supposedly one of the largest exhibition spaces outside London. To the far right (in shadow) is a warehouse complex in Jamaica Street, now restored as the Novas Contemporary Urban Centre.

Heavy-duty plastic strips fall from the rooftop pavilion, a place to see and a place to be seen. The light performs a neat trick here: lighthouse-like, it echoes around multiple surfaces and bounces outwards to announce what the architects have achieved. A beacon, for sure, but also a high nest from which it is possible to see to the river, across to the city and all around this dockland district. Industrial materials respond to the original use of the buildings, but these structures remain subservient to the verve of contemporary imagination. This is the ideal venue for art – the mundane architecture of 1930s dock-related manufacturing is mute and helpless as new work fills these spaces and clambers atop them. The distance, here, between tribute and abuse is smaller than one would like. If it is an abuse, then perhaps the trauma is useful. There would be no meaning here without the efforts of the imagination, just an unremarkable clutch of scraps that say something – but what? – about the past.

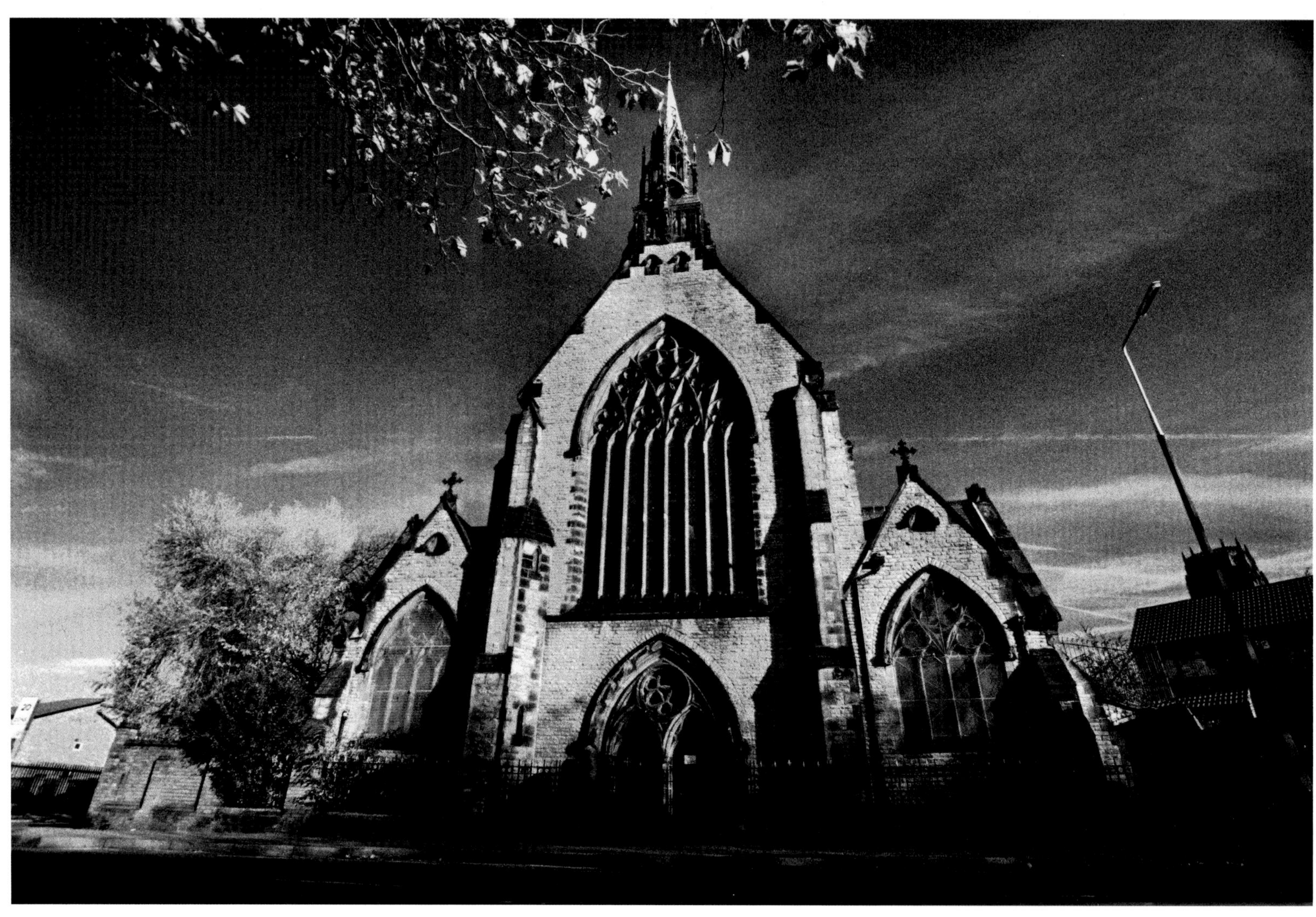

NOVEMBER 2006

St Vincent de Paul Roman Catholic Church, Edward Welby Pugin, 1856–57

Stark and authoritative, Pugin's church muscles its way right to the building line of St James Street, except that decades of bombing, clearance and re-housing schemes have left it with no other buildings along the street for company. The cliff-like solemnity of this western elevation is relieved by the playful timber bellcote at the tip, its light, geometric fretwork acting as an almost independent piece of sculpture suspended in the air. Catholicism was a huge part of dockland culture, and this building dates from the time of rapid expansion of the Catholic population following mass Irish immigration. Although forming part of a living parish community, the church, as a building at least, is also a solemn monument to a life now past. Enduring much in the past 150 years as it has done, there can be little doubt that Pugin's brooding work will continue to form part of the multicultural patchwork here into the distant future.

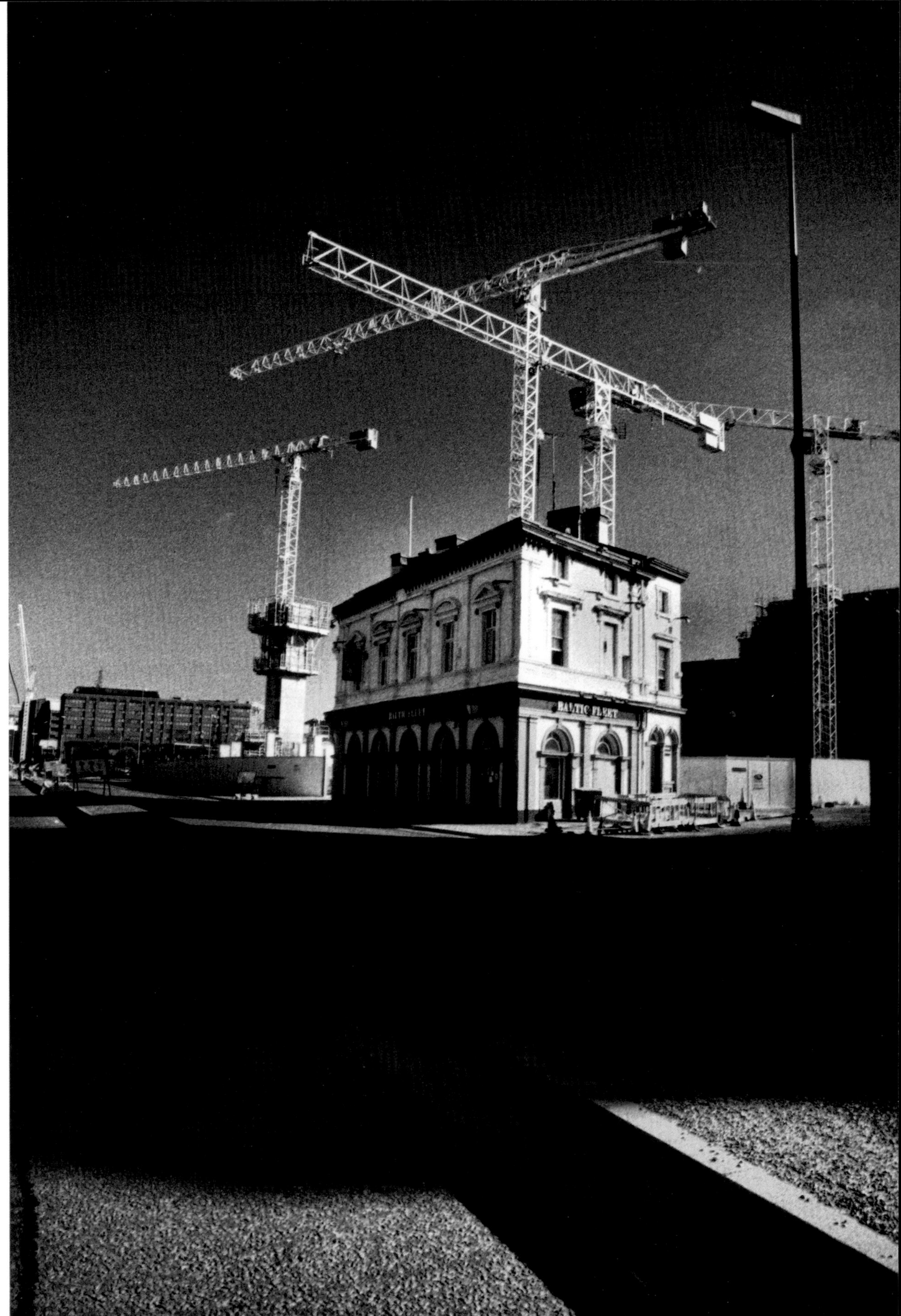

JULY 2006

The Baltic Fleet pub, an heroic survival of the mid-nineteenth-century streetscape along Wapping, stands solid amid the smooth choreography of the cranes all around.

APRIL 2007

Foreground: Fence, pilings and lift tower for hotel and leisure complex on Wapping
Background, from left to right: Hotel Ibis/Formule 1; Heap's Rice Mill; warehousing and warehouse conversions on Cornhill.

A nineteenth-century collection of warehousing is joined by contemporary developments to produce the skyline of a city in miniature. Construction hoardings are a city wall, protecting and emphasising scale. In this light, there is little to distinguish between the smooth shuttered concrete of the various components of contemporary development and the sheer brick walls of the older warehouses. In concert with the opulent development of the banks and offices of the central business district, these were the streets that announced a different type of metropolis, one in which bald functionality was sufficient to create grandeur. This new construction suggests a revival of the same idea; regardless of its intrinsic architectural quality, a return to the scale and density of the nineteenth century in this rebuilding is certainly a welcome change from the ill-advised decimation of the 1980s.

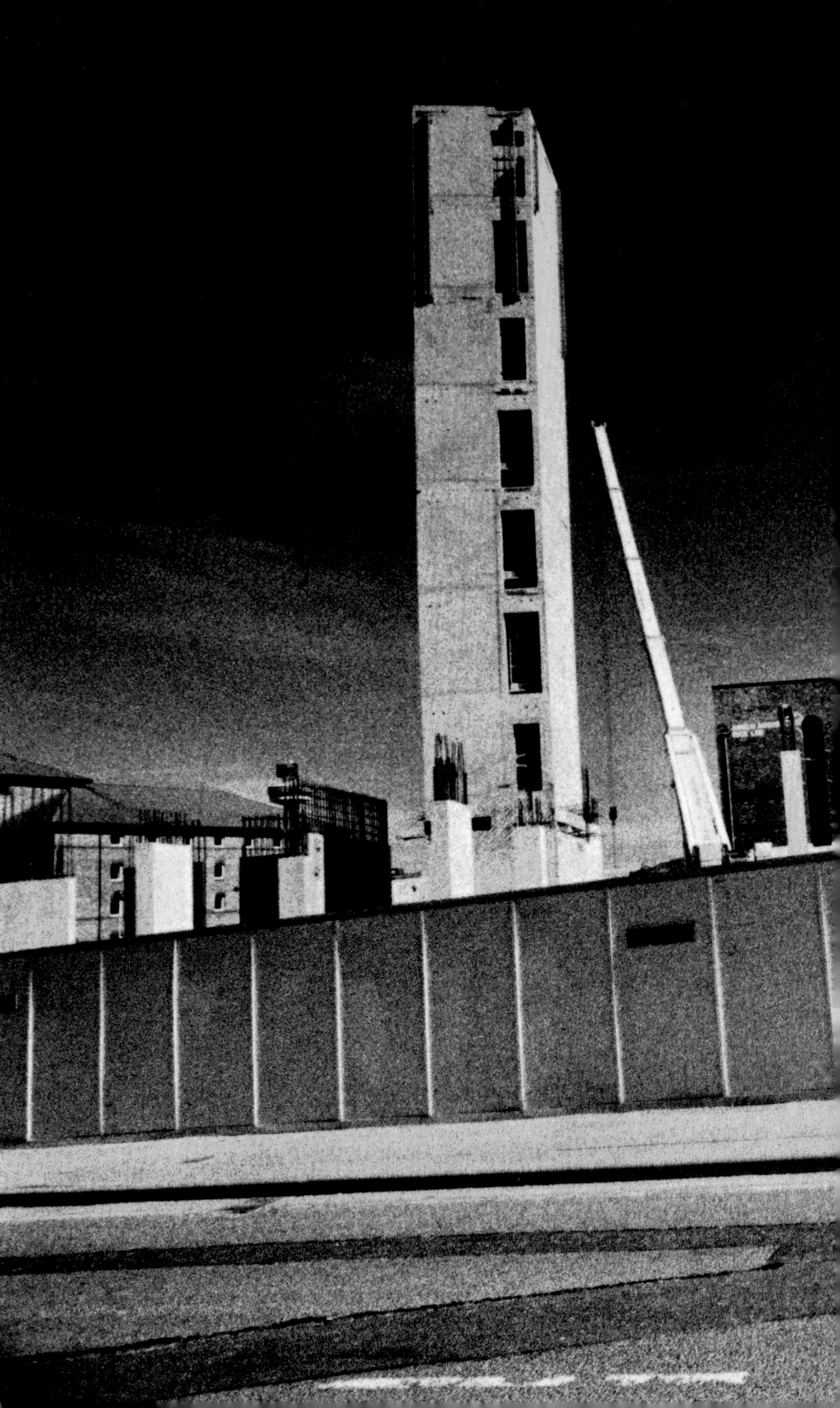

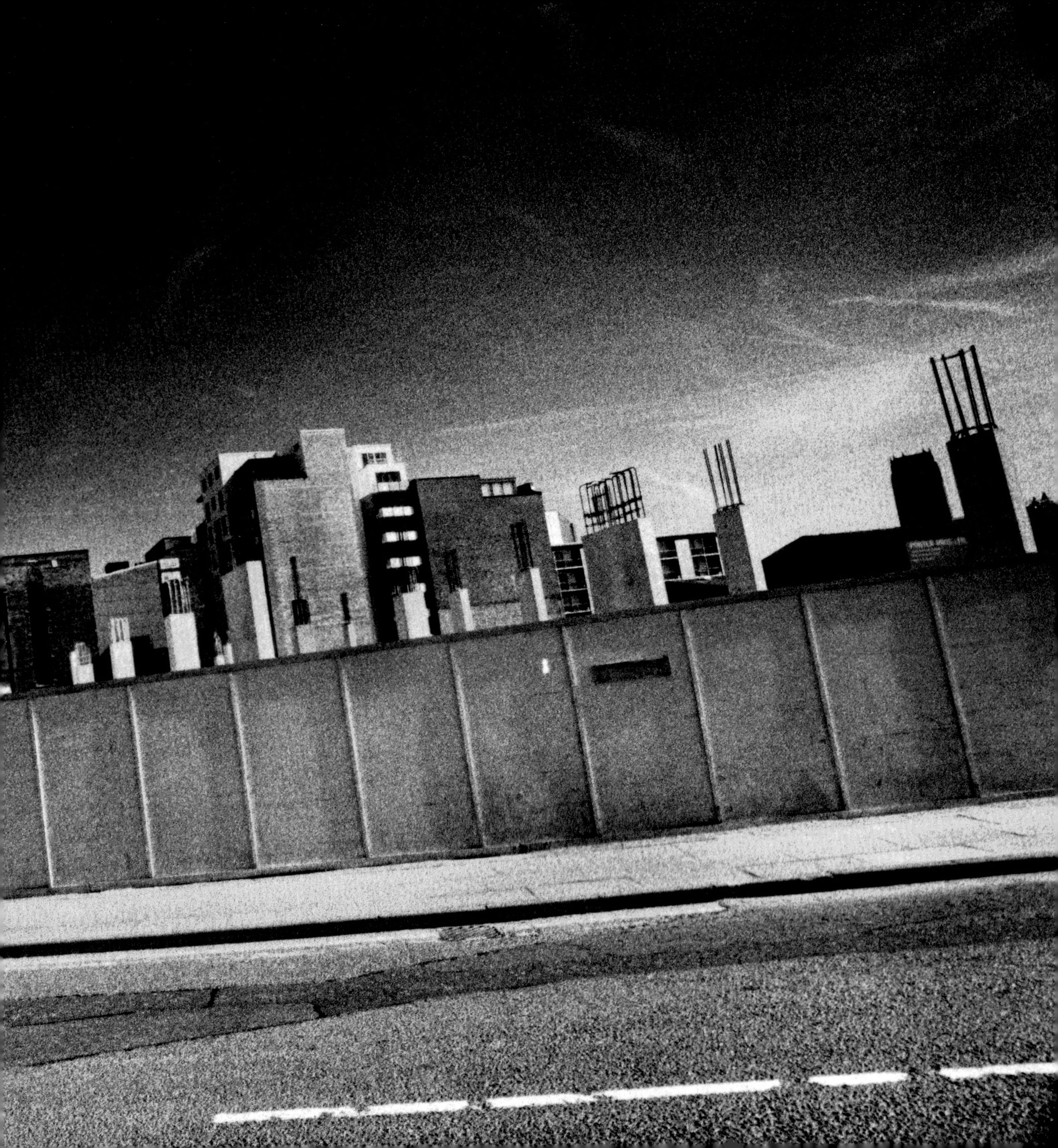

Paradise

Here is a delicate operation; a piece of architectural theatre that must do its work, replacing the parts that the city has lost so that when the stitching is complete and the curtain raised there is a fresh urban scene to behold. This is not a new for old replacement but instead the excavation of a disfigured wound, so altered by age that only a new idea will work here. The cuts are deep, and the implements are heavy, for this is major work. Reaching down into the rock heart of Liverpool, traces of the past are happened upon, acknowledged, and then metamorphosed into a form that can be utilised in the future of this site. An artefact to be top-lit and accompanied by explanatory text; the line of a street to be loosely interpreted afresh; forgotten names to be reused; a place remembered, misremembered, a new place with an idea of the old.

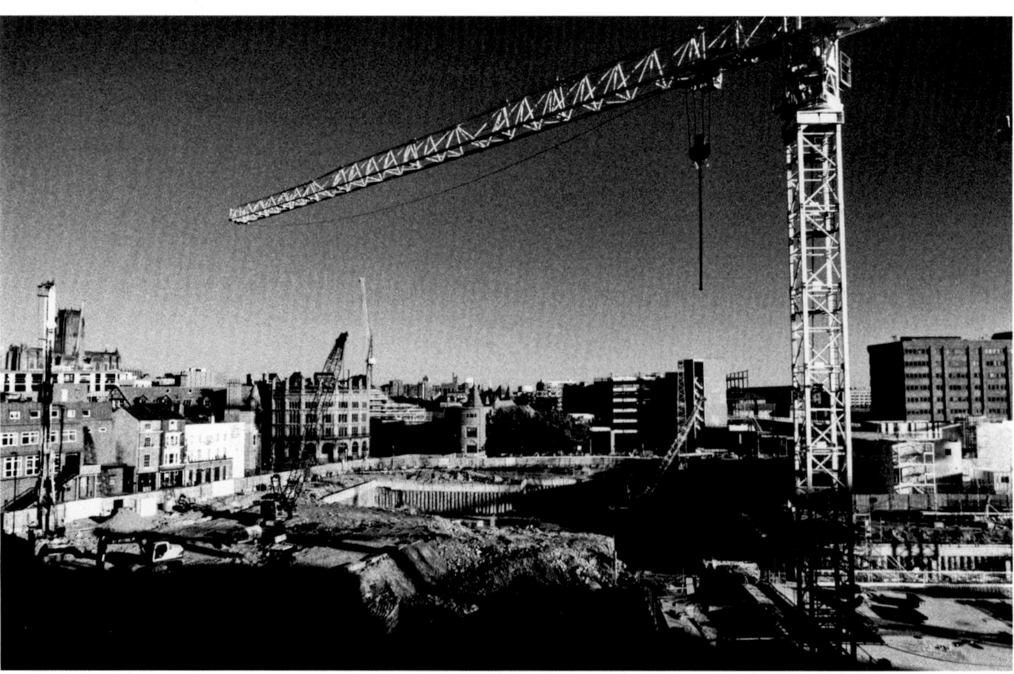

The site of the operation has been, in a sense, prepared and waiting for more than sixty years. The German bombers of May 1941 attacked the very heart of the city, aiming their explosives principally at the docks along the river but successfully obliterating a part of the city's core that pre-dated the engineered incursion of the dock system out into the Mersey. This was the commercial cradle of Liverpool, the site of the inland tidal pool that allowed boats to shelter from the vacillations of the river and made a medieval fishing port a viable site for military and trading excursions. After 1715 this area had at its heart the first enclosed commercial wet dock in the world – a modern engineering solution by Thomas Steers to the tidal extremes that were affecting the efficacy of the burgeoning port. This was an innovation with an almost unimaginable profundity. Technology and sheer will coupled for commercial advantage, nothing more; the profit principle in raw action. This principle did not betray itself, either, for Steers' dock was long gone by the time of the arrival of the Luftwaffe, superseded by the larger docks that took the city further out into the river, replaced by other accoutrements of trade and commerce. A Customs House, shops, warehouses, pubs, dwellings and countless other threads in the weft of a dockland streetscape; all were razed by the aggression of war and few were properly replaced, a sign that Liverpool's *raison d'être*, the power of which had prompted the construction of a unique dock in 1715, was, by the latter half of the twentieth century, losing its strength.

Here is a belated renewal for the twenty-first century, the significance of which cannot be underestimated. This is indeed the scene of Liverpool's beginnings, geographically close to its oldest heart but ideologically at the head of everything else. A new story written on the oldest and most treasured paper. But more than this, the Paradise Project is large and highly visible, and for the majority of its citizens and visitors represents the clearest sign of the successful regeneration of Liverpool. This part of the city cannot be missed, sandwiched in between the existing shopping area and the waterfront. If the heart of our cities is where we buy and dine and perambulate, then this is an entirely new heart for Liverpool.

The tides that rose and fell here along the muddy creek running the length of Paradise Street have found a new expression in an impressive flow of investment, buildings and confidence. As the waters of the Mersey were harnessed for the technological advancement of the port, so the merry-go-round of global capital has been successfully stopped here for some Liverpudlian passengers to embark. Commercial activity on this site has now switched from importing and exporting by sea to retailing goods over counters, but perhaps the economic sensibility is largely the same. There may be reasonable concerns that for Liverpool to replace the romance of international trade with the banal glamour of shopping is to dilute the essence of the city, but this is misguided. The physical flow of goods in and out of Liverpool has not been diminished just because the port has moved downstream of the city centre, far from it; yet now a swelling number of retail outlets at the city's old dockland core are re-invigorating the uncomplicated joys of choosing and acquiring wares from around the world. In the global boom of the early twenty-first century, shopping has assumed the role of image-maker for an entire economy. If the shops and their goods are sleek, well lit and attractively laid out with more than a hint of quality, then all must be well. For too long Liverpool has been excluded from this process, a startling absence in a city with the architecture, style and verve to elevate shopping beyond the mundane. The Paradise Project, committed to streets, urbanity, mass transit, architecture, heritage – all those things that speak of life and a vital culture – seeks to elevate the city back into the national consciousness as a place to shop. This is categorically not a shopping mall, numbed and regulated; it is a piece of a city in development, albeit a piece dedicated to consumption.

Here is a gamble on the present, a chance to develop comprehensively now at the expense of the frisson of future possibilities. There is loss here, as well as growth. For such a very long time, empty land has been covered with broken bricks and grass, while port-associated buildings of the 1800s and 1900s stood stoically against neglect and the elements. For decades, half the charm of Liverpool seemed to reside in the fact that its triumphs were past, its streetscapes and buildings so grand and dilapidated, its scope for renewal so large and unlikely. The historic buildings within the bounds of the scheme are not forgotten in the rush for the new, but instead preened back into a vibrant life. Warehouses for the selling rather than the storing of wares. The latent energy of the ruin is gone, to be replaced by a new hope that energy can be found on these streets again. The romance of melancholy swapped for the prosaic success of occupied buildings, jobs, cleaned bricks and even surfaces. Pragmatically, it is an exchange worth making. For the spirit of the city, it is more of a calculated gamble. This is the chance to regenerate; this is the chance to survive. May it be a worthwhile survival, and one that brings greater glories.

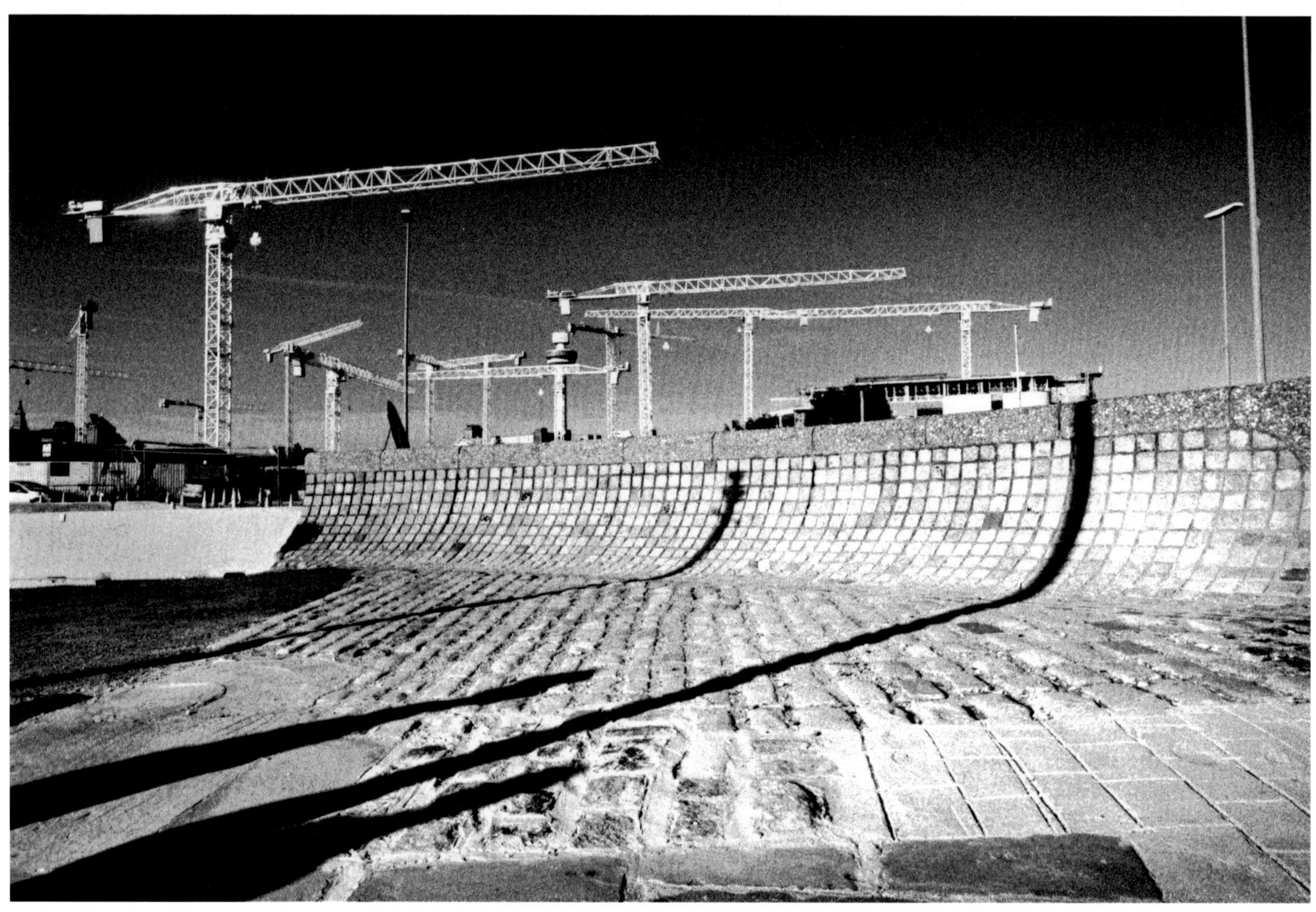

JULY 2006

Viewed from Strand Street, the entire Paradise development area is demarcated by the battle positions of cranes, an advancing army changing this territory forever.

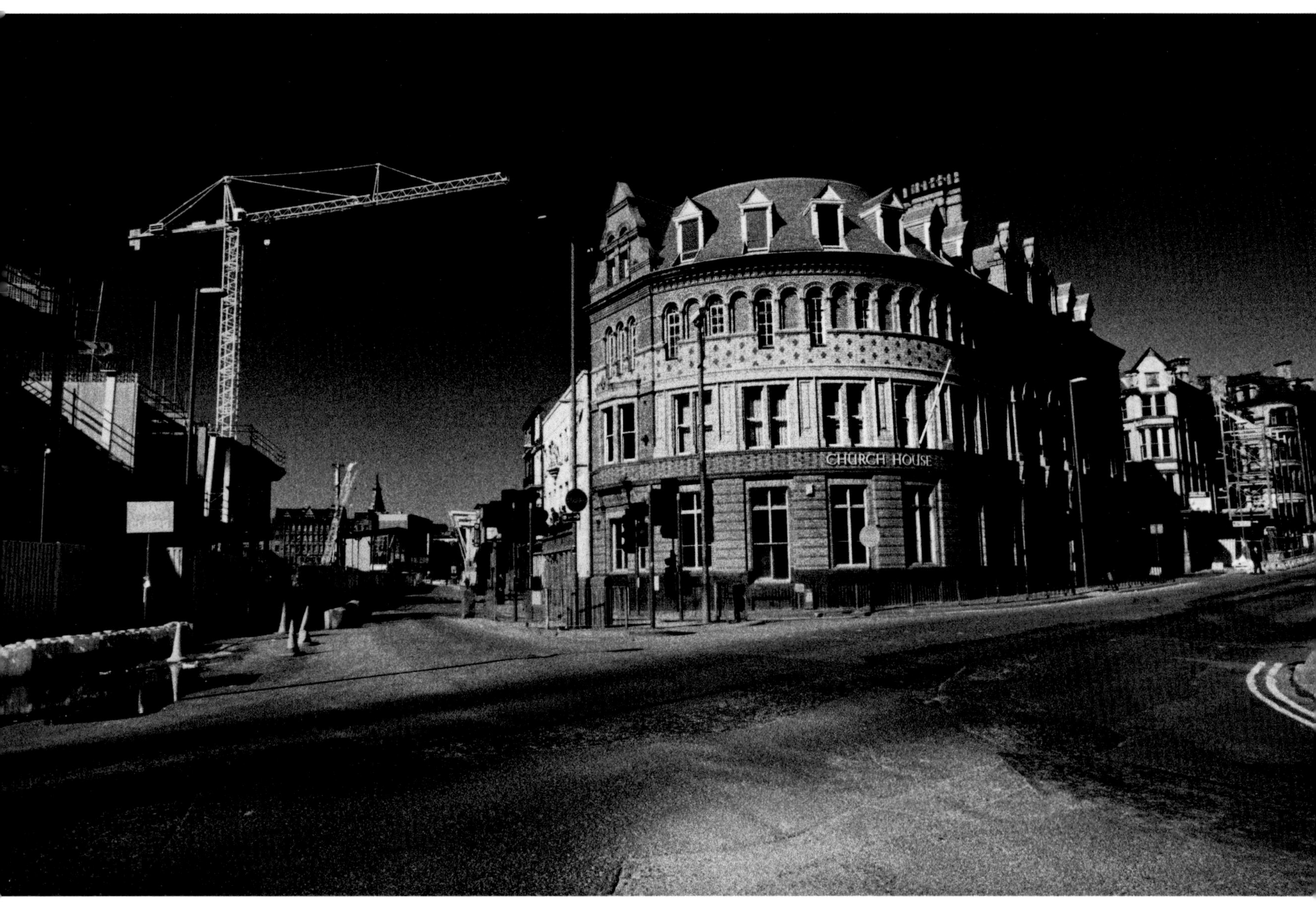

AUGUST 2005

From left to right: Construction on Paradise Street; Church House, George Enoch Grayson, opened 1885 as the Mersey Mission to Seamen and temperance pub; former Hanover Galleries; Stanley buildings

As Paradise Street is almost completely rebuilt from the ground up, Church House and the rescued Victorian warehouses along Hanover Street stand assuredly into the future.

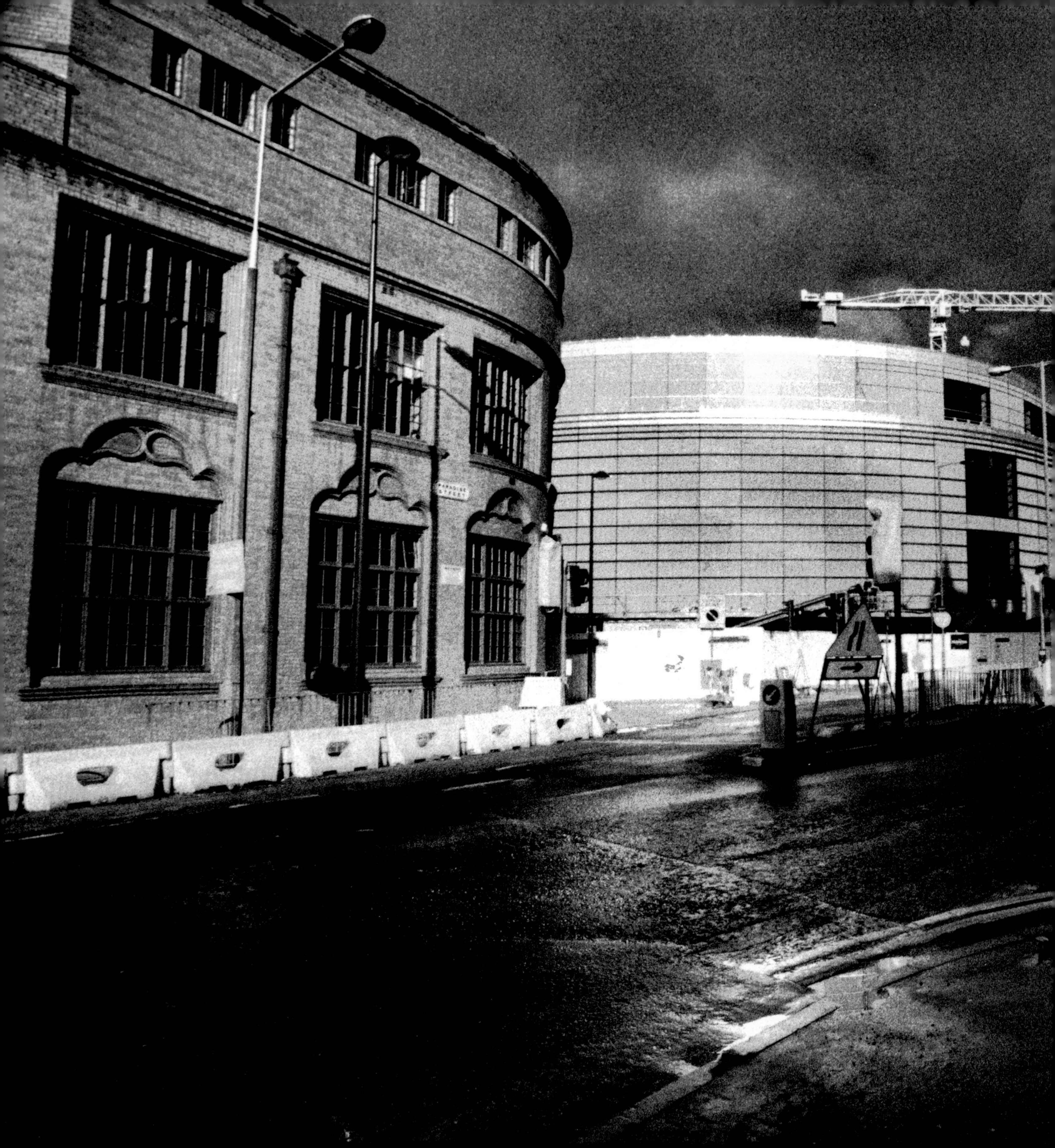
PARADISE
STREET

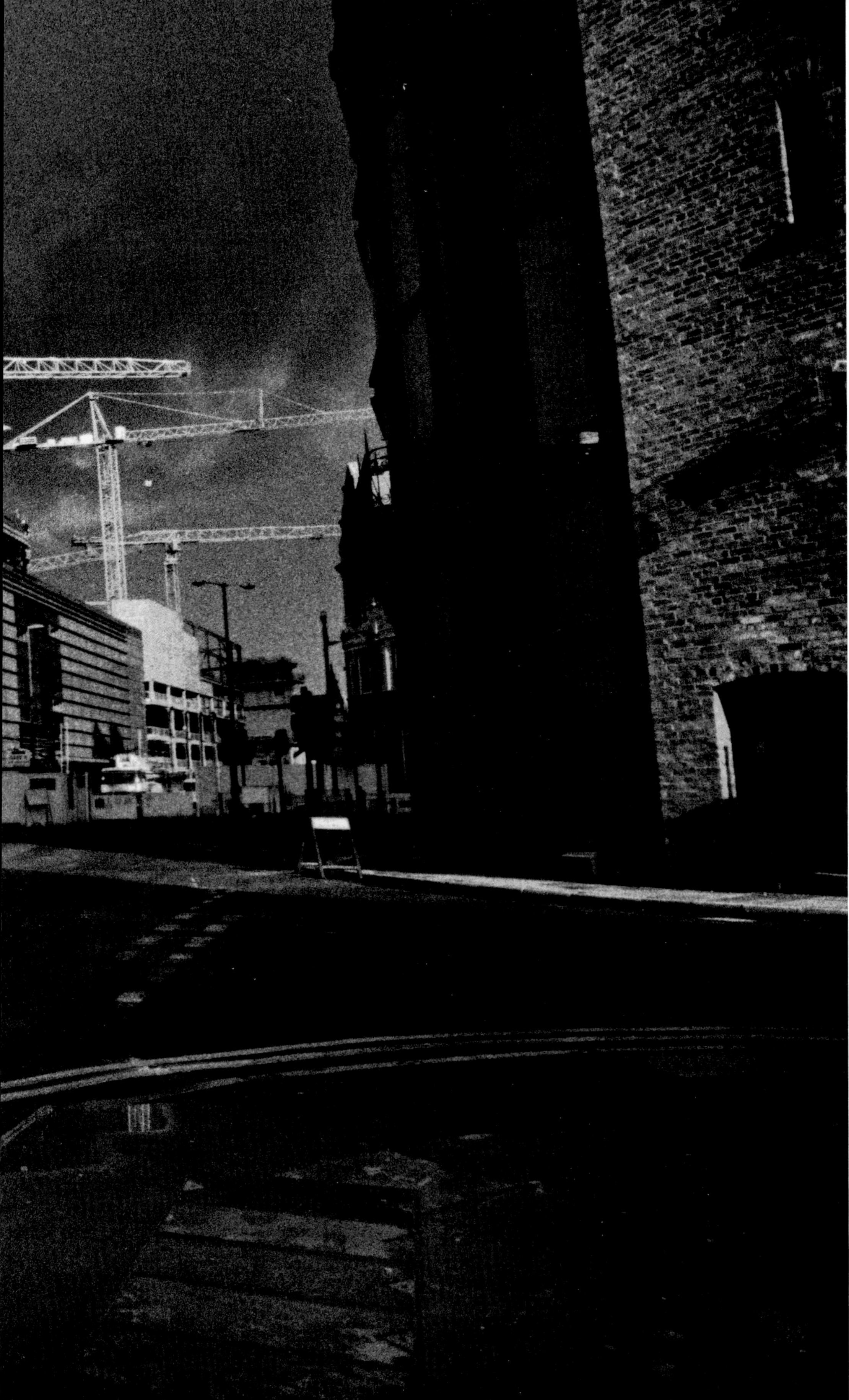

NOVEMBER 2006

From left to right: Chancery House, James Strong, 1899, built as the Gordon Smith Institute for Seamen, incorporating library, assembly hall and reading room, now offices; John Lewis department store, John McAslan & Partners, 2004–08

John Lewis holds its new corner site, edging forward to meet the gothic certainties that have held counsel here for a century or more. Now all is reflection, shimmer and shadow, an appropriate impermanence in the face of the bold cityscape and bolder ideas of another time.

The city here remains on hold. Traffic lights are masked before use. Liverpool stops and waits, its upheaval demands this frozen time, energy preserved for the metamorphosis. The traffic will come, the people and the cars, and flow over this junction. The new edifices will reflect and shimmer with life. The old will remain.

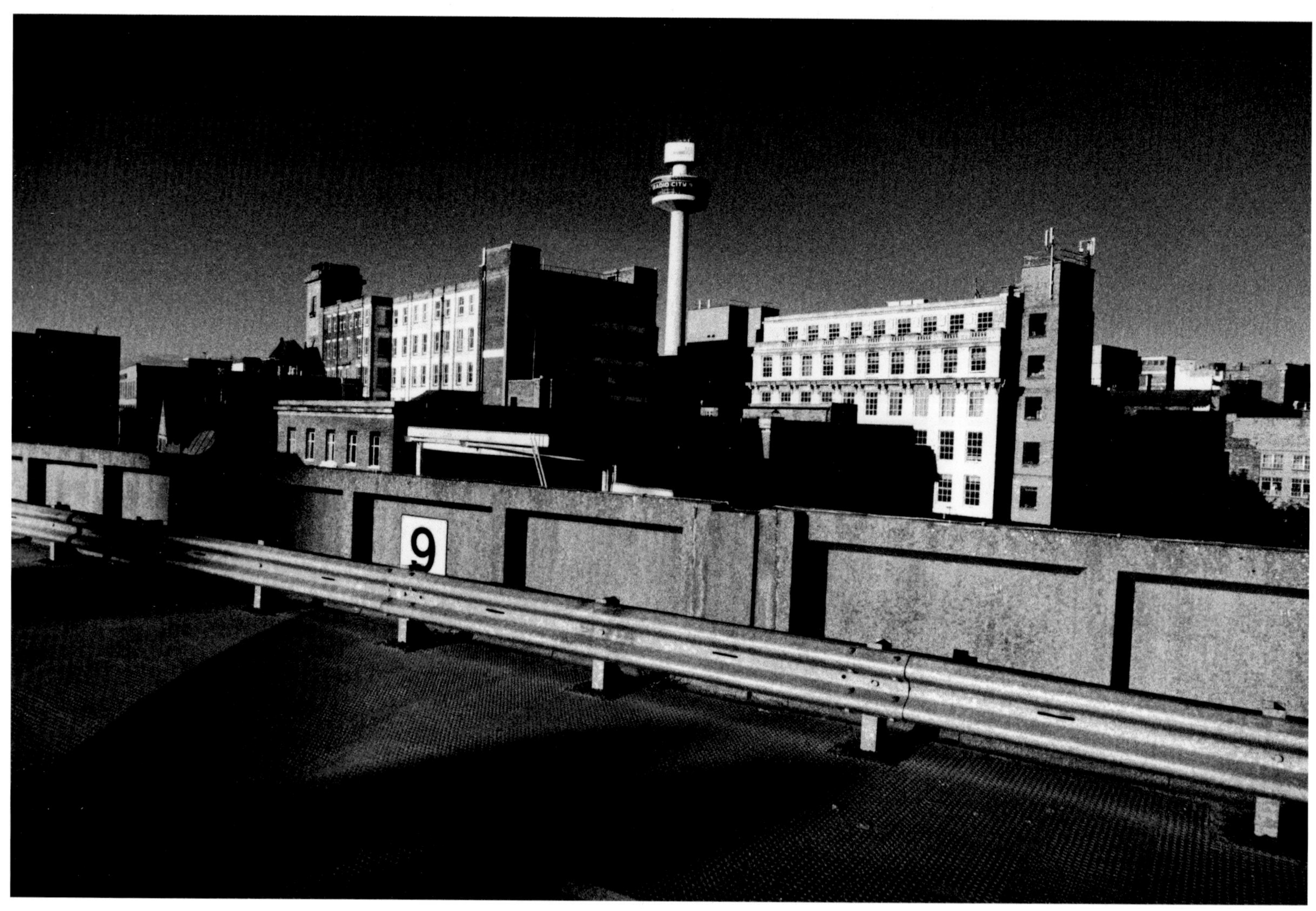

AUGUST 2005

From the top of the now-demolished NCP car park on Paradise Street, the city reveals a trans-Atlantic face. From the prosaic asphalt of the multi-storey, a forest of structures sets the scene. These forms, with classical detailing overlaid onto functional buildings, create a cityscape of elegant modernity.

St John's Beacon, meanwhile, explicitly echoes the space-age modernity of the 1960s to be found in Seattle or Toronto. These massed blocks and sombre shadows recall a certain east-coast noir, a fairytale of New York in which an unapologetic urbanism acts as the backdrop for a thousand encounters.

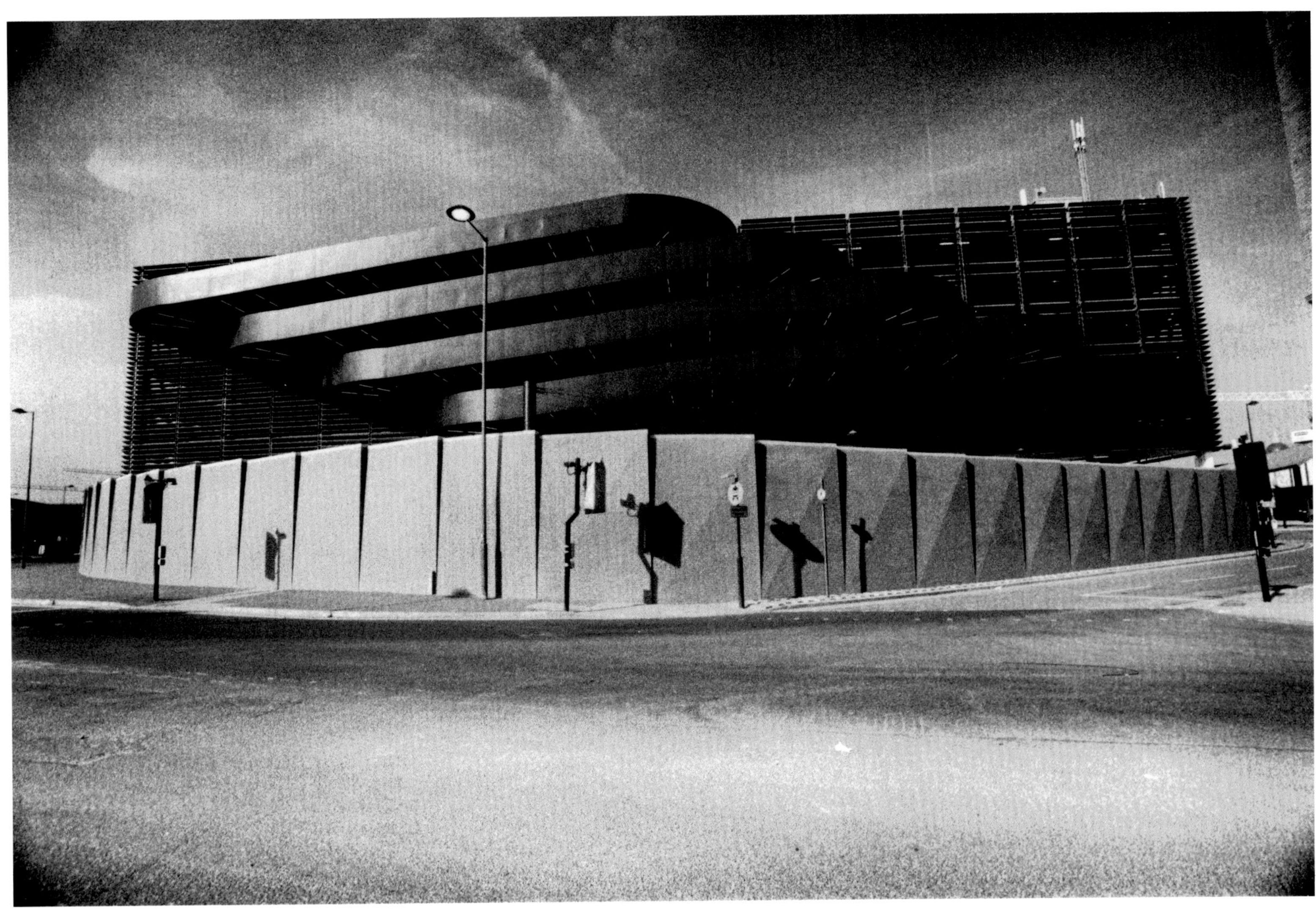

NOVEMBER 2005

Liver Street car park, Wilkinson Eyre, 2004–05

The new Liver Street car park picks up the autumnal sunlight on its external ramps. One of the first projects to be completed within the overall Paradise Street development scheme, this is a building that innovates way beyond the basic demands of its function to provide parking spaces for the new John Lewis store. Both citadel and sculpture, this holds an expressiveness that need not be there. Undoubtedly it is there, and so the first shoots of growth in Liverpool's retail regeneration have brought forth that rarest of forms – a car park that is not depressing.

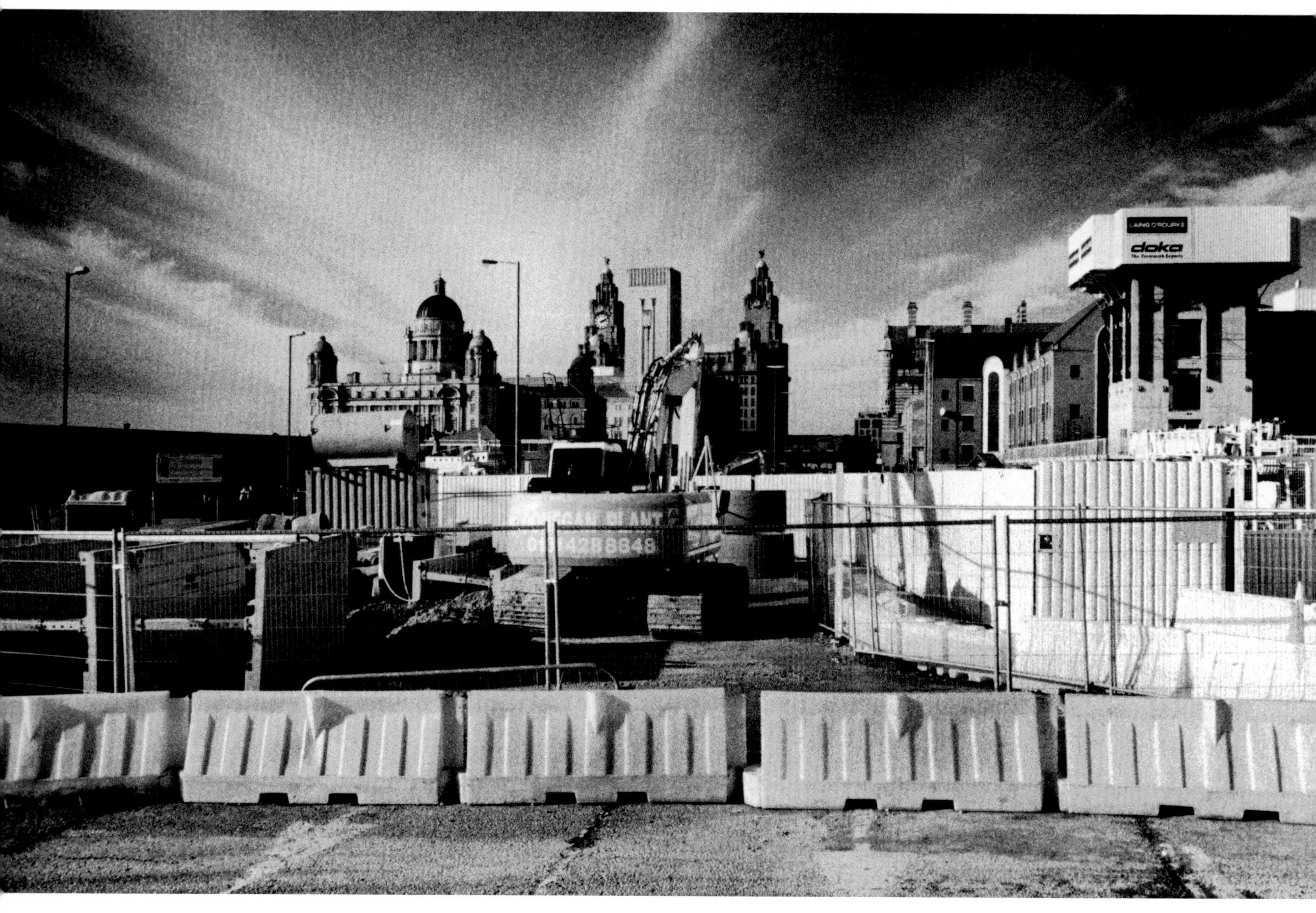

FEBRUARY 2007

Background from left to right: Port of Liverpool Building (formerly offices of the Mersey Docks and Harbour Board), Briggs and Wolstenhome/Hobbs and Thornley, 1903–07; Royal Liver Building, Walter Aubrey Thomas, 1908–11; George's Dock Ventilation Tower and Control Station, Herbert J. Rowse, 1932–34; former offices of the White Star Line, Norman Shaw with James F. Doyle, 1895–98; offices for HBOS plc, 1990s

Foreground: Temporary fencing and construction plant on Strand Street

DECEMBER 2004

Background: 12 Hanover Street, former offices and warehousing for Ellis & Co., shipowners and merchants, Edmund Kirby, 1899–91. Earlier warehouse of 1863 to the right, turning into Argyle Street

Gables and pinnacles stand proudly in the sky, overlooking the old dockland streetscape. The temporary sentinels of traffic control demarcate a new way. Change swirls all around yet the markers of the old remain; tall, and blasted into near permanence with terracotta and brick.

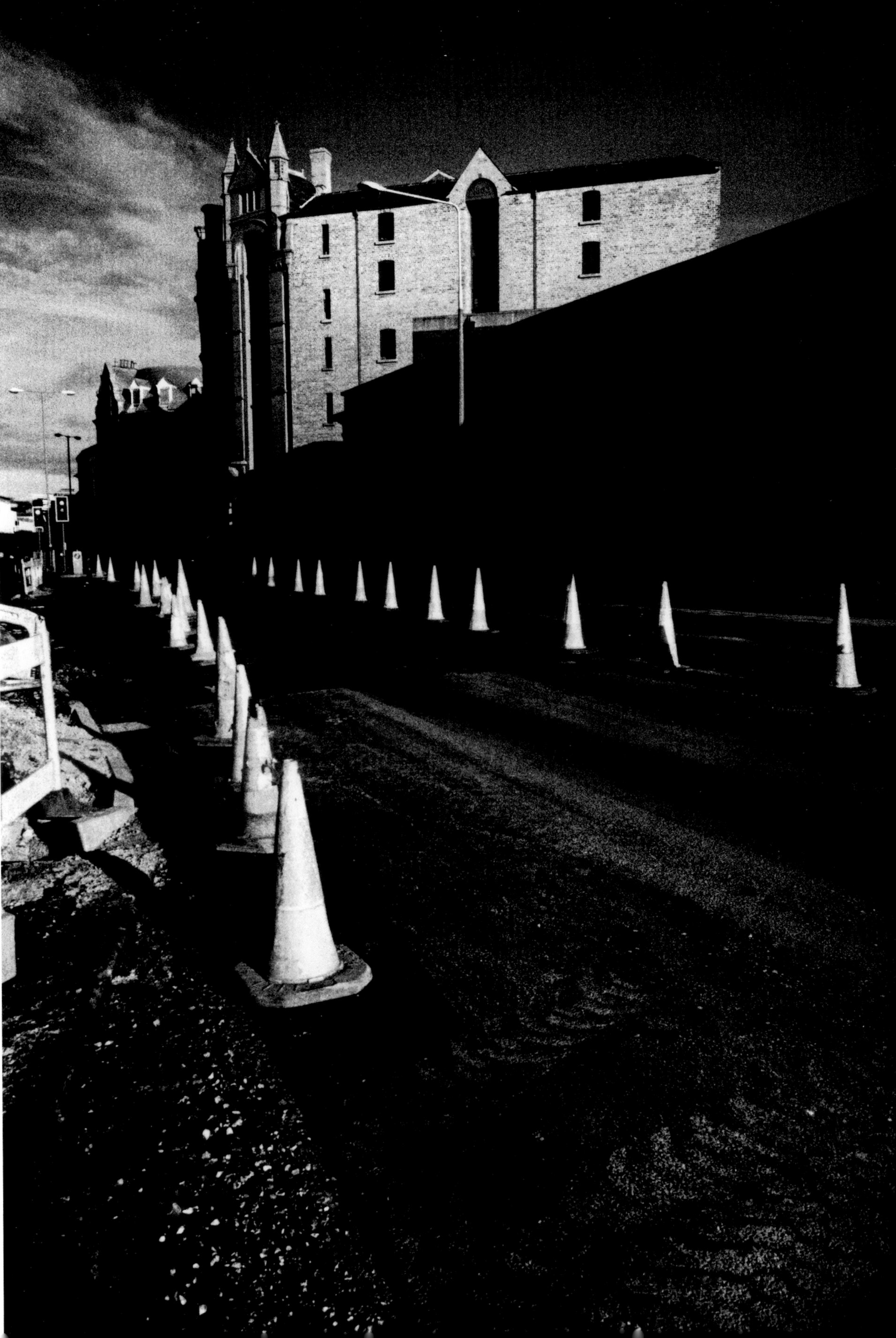

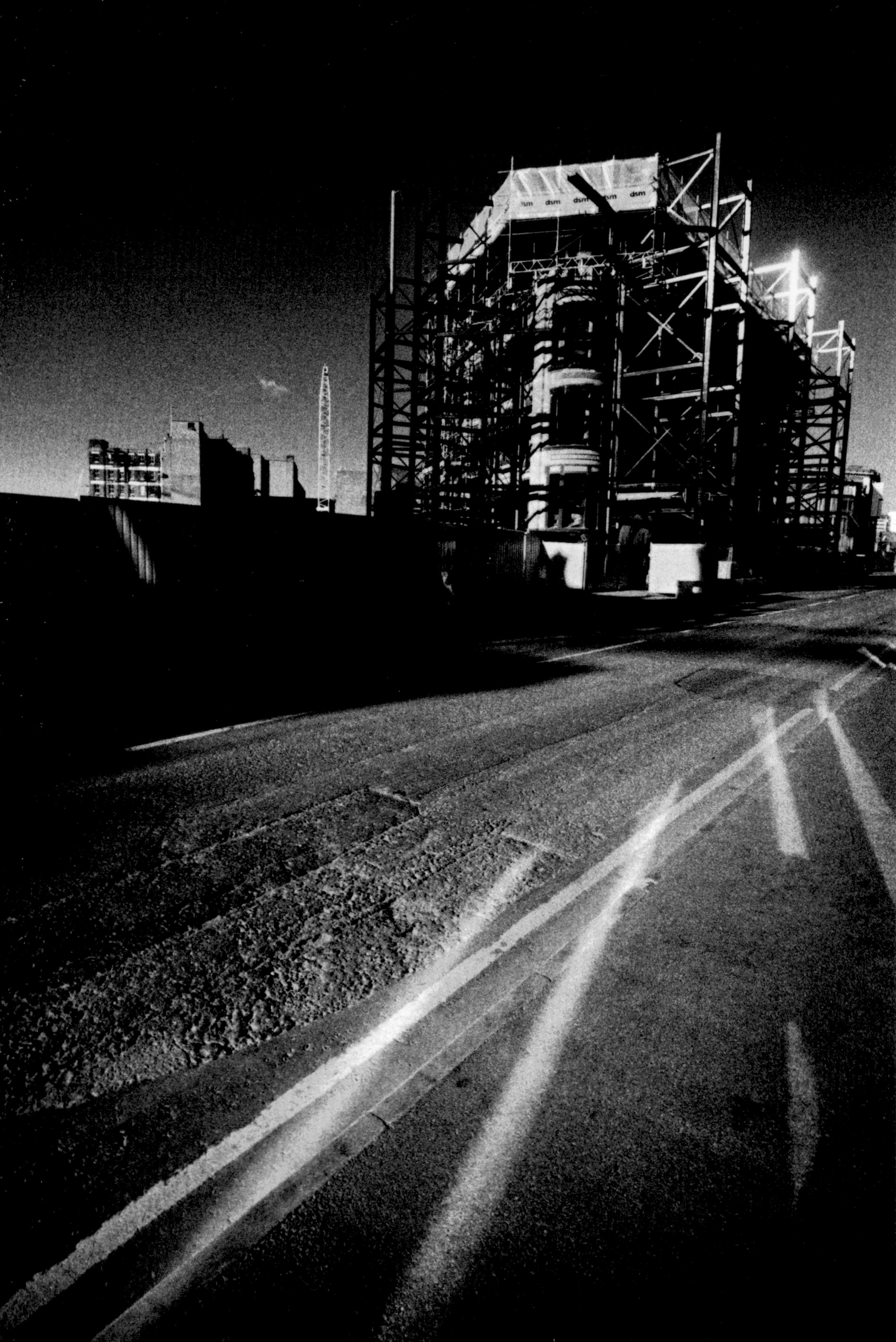

SEPTEMBER 2006

The devastation of demolition leaves precious fragments to be preserved at all costs. Cocooned in a scaffold that more closely resembles a standing structure than a support, this nineteenth-century warehouse, Stanley Buildings, has been earmarked for salvation from the very beginning of the plan for Paradise. Gestating inside the superstructure, this heritage shell will be strengthened and refitted with suitable innards so that it may make its own contribution to the new streetscape and economic life of Hanover Street.

JUNE 2008

One Park West, César Pelli, 2006–08

The major residential building in the Paradise redevelopment area, Pelli's creation frames one side of Chavasse Park with a crescent of glass rising to the drama of a chamfered corner and blade-sharp pinnacle. This is all a welcome return to the sort of scale that warehouses once provided along Strand Street, albeit in a more glamorous manifestation.

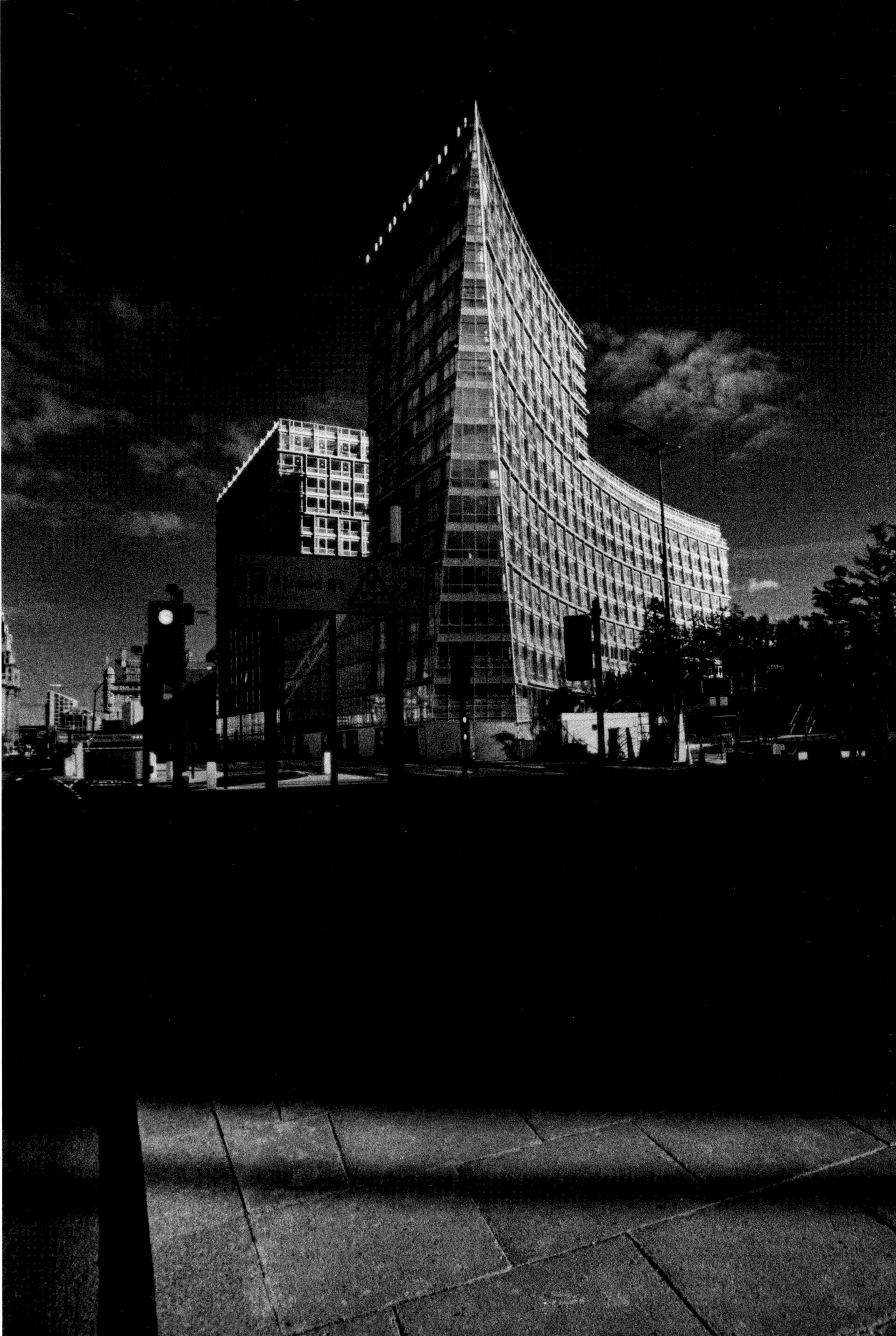

ALAN MCKERNAN

A lecturer in photography at Liverpool Community College for many years, Alan's previous books include *Unfamiliar Journeys*, a photo-essay on Liverpool's architectural richness, and *Sea Margins*, an evocative exploration of the landscapes along the Formby coastline published in collaboration with the National Trust.

Alan continues to study the varying effects of light using the traditional medium of silver-based black and white photography, combined with specialist hand-printing techniques, to produce hauntingly atmospheric images that re-draw our perceptions of Liverpool.

MATTHEW WHITFIELD

Matthew is an architectural historian who was born and educated in Liverpool. He was the winner of the *Hawksmoor* essay medal for 2006, awarded by the Society of Architectural Historians of Great Britain, and has written for *Twentieth Century Architecture*, the journal of the Twentieth Century Society.